Diabetic Air Fryer Cookbook

Iris Mason

Table of Contents

CHAPTER 7. MEAT RECIPES 76

CHAPTER 8. DESSERT RECIPES 97

Introduction

Diabetes has become widespread in our society. This disease affects millions of people and can be fatal if not managed properly. Fortunately, there are things you can do to control blood sugar levels. One of the best ways is the use of an air fryer. This guide will explain how air fryers are used for a diabetic diet and how they could help you. You will also learn how to make diabetic recipes using an air fryer. There are numerous benefits to the diabetic diet, but we need to learn about diabetic cooking.

The air fryer offers health benefits for those with diabetes. People with diabetes have to watch their diet and monitor their blood sugar levels. The *Diabetic Air Fryer Cookbook* gives a step-by-step guide to preparing healthy meals and snacks in the air fryer. This explains the benefits of a diabetic diet, how to use air fryers properly, and what people with diabetes are supposed to eat. When you have diabetes, you must change your eating habits to help keep your blood sugar levels under control. You will lower your chances of getting heart disease and stroke by eating healthy foods and controlling high blood sugar levels with medication. Several types of food may not be safe for you, depending on which type of diabetes you have.

Many different types of diabetes can make your blood sugar spike, but often the diet that causes it is not known. This will teach you how to use an air fryer to control your diabetes with a low-carb diet. Many myths surround the air fryer, but they all prove to be wrong once you take a deeper look at them. People believe that because the foods cooked in an air fryer are unhealthy, they should never be used for diabetes. This is a myth as the air fryer can cook quite well without compromising on taste and flavor. The air fryer is a powerful kitchen equipment that allows you to cook food in a healthier way than regular cooking methods. You can use your air fryer for cooking foods traditionally fried or baked at lower temperatures and without any unhealthy fat or oil. This allows you to enjoy more variety in your diet and experience amazing tasting results.

You will find many different recipes that fit into your diabetic diet. You will learn how to include air-fried foods in your diet while maintaining a low-carb diet. Most of the recipes include high protein and low carbohydrate foods, which keep your blood sugar in check. Most of the recipes are simple to make to add to your daily life easily. You can make all your favorite meals, including fried chicken legs, mashed potatoes, and macaroni and cheese. Because some foods cause glucose to rise too quickly in the bloodstream, and some foods cause glucose to fall too quickly, we understand that the perfect diet for diabetes is not an easy task. However, with a little research and our cookbook, you can make delicious meals without worrying about your meal controlling blood sugar levels.

Not only can you eat like a person with diabetes, but with our recipes, you can also make healthier dishes. This is the perfect solution because they allow you to cook without worrying about what you are going to eat when you are done. This is designed to serve both as an introduction to the air fryer and as a guide to controlling diabetes through diet. You will get to know how easy it is to eat healthier meals by using your air fryer. Your health will thank you for it!

When you would have finished reading this, I invite you to leave a review. This would mean so much to me as it would help the dissemination of this material. I really worked hard on this product; I genuinely hope you like it!

Chapter 1. What Is Diabetes

Diabetes is a disease that affects how your body uses sugar, usually in the form of glucose. Sometimes people with type 1 diabetes do not make enough insulin, and their bodies cannot use the glucose properly. The disease also causes high blood sugar levels and can make it harder for you to control urination or thirst. If left untreated, diabetes can lead to heart, kidney, eye, or nerve damage. If a person has too much sugar in their bloodstream, they can die from diabetic ketoacidosis. The consequences of continued untreated diabetes are an enormous burden on those who are ill and those around them. With proper treatment, the outcome is much better for all involved as long as complications are identified quickly and dealt with accordingly.

Type 1 diabetes is a form of diabetes in which the body's immune system destroys a type of cell in the pancreas called the beta-cells. These cells produce insulin, and without it, the body can't break down food to give energy to muscles, tissues, and cells. Type 2 diabetes is another form of diabetes in which either your body doesn't produce enough insulin or isn't able to use what it produces as well as usual. In both cases, you need more insulin than your own body can possibly produce on its own.

Type 1 vs Type 2 Diabetes

Type 1 diabetes is an autoimmune disease. In cases of type 1 diabetes, the immune system attacks cells in the pancreas responsible for insulin production. Although we are unsure what causes this reaction, many experts believe it is brought upon by a gene deficiency or by viral infections that may trigger the disease.

Type 2 diabetes is a metabolic disorder, although research suggests it may warrant reclassification as an autoimmune disease as well. People who grieve from type 2 diabetes have a high resistance to insulin or an inability to produce enough insulin. Professionals believe that type 2 diabetes is a result of a genetic predisposition in many people, which is further aggravated by obesity and other environmental triggers.

Diagnosis

Diabetes diagnosis has come incredibly far in the last few decades. Currently, there are two primary tests for diagnosing diabetes: the fasting plasma glucose (FPG) test and the hemoglobin A1C test. The FPG test takes your blood sugar levels after an eight-hour fasting period; this helps to show if your body is processing glucose at a healthy rate. The A1C test shows your blood sugar levels over the last three months. It does this by testing the amount of glucose being carried by the hemoglobin of your red blood cells. Hemoglobin has a lifespan of roughly three months; this allows us to test it to see how long it has been carrying glucose and how much it has.

Symptoms of Diabetes Type 1 and 2

In type 1 diabetes, the list of symptoms can be extensive with both serious and less obvious indicators. Below, I will list the most common symptoms as well as other potential complications of type 1 diabetes:

- **Excessive thirst:** Extreme thirst is one of the less noticeable indicators of type 1 diabetes. It is brought upon by high blood sugar (hyperglycemia).
- **Frequent urination:** Frequent urination is caused by your kidneys failing to process all of the glucose in your blood; this forces your body to attempt to flush out excess glucose through urinating.
- **Fatigue:** Fatigue in type 1 diabetes patients is caused by the body's inability to process glucose for energy.

- **Excessive hunger:** Those who have type 1 diabetes often have persistent hunger and increased appetites. This is because the body is desperate for glucose despite its inability to process it without insulin.
- **Cloudy or unclear vision:** Rapid fluctuations in blood sugar levels can lead to cloudy or blurred vision. Those suffering from untreated type 1 diabetes are unable to naturally control their blood sugar levels, making rapid fluctuations a very common occurrence.
- **Rapid weight loss:** Rapid weight loss is probably the most noticeable symptom of type 1 diabetes. As your body starves off glucose, it resorts to breaking down muscle and fat to sustain itself. This can lead to incredibly fast weight loss in type 1 diabetes cases.
- **Ketoacidosis:** Ketoacidosis is a potentially deadly complication of untreated type 1 diabetes. In response to the lack of glucose being fed into your muscles and organs, your body starts breaking down your fat and muscle into an energy source called ketones, which can be burned without the need for insulin. Ketones are usually perfectly fine in normal amounts. But, when your body is starving, it may end up flooding itself with ketones in an attempt to fuel itself; the acidification of your blood that follows this influx of acid molecules may lead to more serious conditions, such as a coma or death.

In cases of type 2 diabetes, the symptoms tend to be slower to develop, and they tend to be mild early on. Some early symptoms mimic type 1 diabetes and may include:

- **Excessive hunger:** Similar to type 1 diabetes, those of us with type 2 diabetes will feel constant hunger. Again, this is brought on by our bodies looking for fuel because of our inability to process glucose.
- **Fatigue and mental fog:** Depending on the severity of the insulin shortage in type 2 sufferers, they may feel physical fatigue and mental fogginess during their average day.
- **Frequent urination:** Another symptom of both type 1 and 2 diabetes. Frequent urination is simply your body's way of attempting to rid itself of excess glucose.
- **Dry mouth and constant thirst:** It is unclear what causes dry mouth in diabetic sufferers, but it is tightly linked to high blood sugar levels. Constant thirst is brought on not only by a dry mouth but also by the dehydration that frequent urination causes.
- **Itchy skin:** Itching of the skin, especially around the hands and feet, is a sign of polyneuropathy (diabetic nerve damage). As well as being a sign of potential nerve damage, itching can be a sign of high concentrations of cytokines circulating in your bloodstream; these are inflammatory molecules that can lead to itching. Cytokines are signaling proteins and hormonal regulators that are often released in high amounts before nerve damage.

As type 2 diabetes progresses and becomes more serious, the symptoms can become highly uncomfortable and dangerous. Some of these advanced symptoms include:

- **Slow healing of bruises, cuts, and abrasions:** Many people suffering from type 2 diabetes have impaired immune systems due to the lack of energy available to the body. As well as a lack of energy, many diabetics have slowed circulation brought upon by high blood glucose levels. Both of these factors lead to a much slower healing process and far greater risks of infection.
- **Yeast infections:** For women with type 2 diabetes, the chances of yeast infections are far higher than in non-diabetic women. This is due to high blood sugar levels and a lowered immune system response.
- **Neuropathy or numbness:** Long-term high blood sugar levels can lead to severe nerve damage in adults with diabetes. It is believed around 70% of people with type 2 diabetes have some form of neuropathy (Hoskins, 2020). Diabetic neuropathy is characterized by numbness in the extremities, specifically around the feet and fingers.

- **Dark skin patches (acanthosis nigricans):** Some people with type 2 diabetes may have far above normal levels of insulin in their blood as their body is unable to utilize it due to insulin resistance. This rise of insulin in the bloodstream can lead to some skin cells reproducing and cause black patches to form on the skin.

Complications

Severe complications of diabetes can be debilitating and deadly. Both type 1 & type 2 diabetes can cause serious neurological, cardiovascular, and optical conditions. Some of the most common complications of advanced diabetes are as follows:

- **Heart attacks:** Diabetes is directly linked to a higher rate of heart attacks in adults. High blood glucose levels damage the cells and nerves around the heart and blood vessels over time, which can cause a plethora of heart diseases to form.
- **Cataracts:** People with diabetes have a nearly 60% greater chance of developing cataracts later in life if their diabetes is left unchecked (Diabetes.co.uk, 2019a). Doctors are not sure of the real reason for cataracts forming at a higher rate in diabetes patients, but many believe it has to do with the lower amounts of glucose available to the cells powering our eyes.
- **Peripheral artery disease (PAD):** This is a very common case of diabetes, and it causes decreased blood flow, which leads to serious issues in the lower legs, often resulting in amputation.
- **Diabetic nephropathy:** Diabetic nephropathy happens when high levels of blood glucose damage parts of your kidneys, which are responsible for filtering blood. This causes your kidneys to develop chronic kidney diseases and break down over time, leading to failure.
- **Glaucoma:** Diabetes can cause glaucoma in sufferers due to high blood sugar levels, and this directly damages blood vessels in the eyes. When your body attempts to repair these vessels, it may cause glaucoma on the iris where the damage was caused.

10 Tips to Control Diabetes

- **Eat less salt:** Salt can increase your chances of having high blood pressure, which leads to increased chances of heart disease and stroke.
- **Replace sugar:** Replace sugar with zero-calorie sweeteners. Cutting out sugar gives you much more control over your blood sugar levels.
- **Cut out alcohol:** Alcohol tends to be high in calories, and if drunk on an empty stomach with insulin medication, it can cause drastic drops in blood sugar.
- **Be physically active:** Physical action decreases your risk of cardiovascular issues and increases your body's natural glucose burn rate.
- **Avoid saturated fats:** Saturated fats like butter and pastries can lead to high cholesterol and blood circulation issues.
- **Use canola or olive oil:** If you need to use oil in your cooking, use canola or olive oil. Both are high in beneficial fatty acids and monounsaturated fat.
- **Drink water:** Water is by far the healthiest drink you can have. Drinking water helps to regulate blood sugar and insulin levels.
- **Make sure you get enough vitamin D:** Vitamin D is a crucial vitamin for controlling blood sugar levels. Eat food high in this vitamin or ask your doctor about supplements.
- **Avoid processed food:** Processed foods tend to be high in vegetable oils, salt, refined grains, or other unhealthy additives.
- **Drink coffee and tea:** Not only are coffee and tea great hunger suppressants for dieters, but they contain important antioxidants that help with protecting cells.

How to Prevent Diabetes

Diabetes mellitus is a disease that affects our metabolism. The predominant characteristic of diabetes is an inability to create or utilize insulin, a hormone that moves sugar from our blood cells into the rest of our body's cells. This is crucial for us because we rely on that blood sugar to power our body and provide energy. High blood sugar, if not treated, can lead to serious damage to our eyes, nerves, kidneys, and other major organs. There are 2 main types of diabetes, they are type 1 and type 2, with the second being the most common of the two with over 90% of diabetics suffering from it.

Insulin resistance is the most popular cause of type 2 diabetes. Because muscle, fat, and liver cells no longer respond to insulin, the pancreas secretes a lot of it in order to keep blood sugar levels in check. Insulin resistance is exacerbated by being overweight and physically sedentary.

Prediabetes and glucose intolerance both cause insulin resistance. Prediabetes affects an estimated 79 million Americans. According to studies, decreasing 7% of your body weight and exercising regularly can reduce your risk of type 2 diabetes by 58%. Insulin resistance can be reduced by decreasing weight, exercising regularly, eating carbohydrates in moderation, and eating a nutritious diet once you've been diagnosed with diabetes. As a result, better blood sugar control will be achieved.

Type 2 diabetes is the most common form of the disease in adults. As we age, our cells don't use insulin as well and, therefore, cannot convert glucose into energy. The condition also increases your risk for serious health risks like heart disease, blindness, kidney failure, amputations, and stroke.

The first step in preventing diabetes is to know what the risk factors are. It all starts with your levels of glucose in the blood. This can be measured by two methods: fasting plasma glucose test and random plasma glucose test.

The number one cause of diabetes is a family history: people who have a parent or sibling with type 1 or type 2 diabetes are likely to develop it themselves. If you want to lower your own risk, avoid early pregnancies, limit weight gain during pregnancy and breastfeed for at least two years. Also, know your glycemic index to help you lose weight.

The next step is to start eating right and exercising regularly.

- **Eat a balanced diet:** Eat vegetables, whole grains, fruits, nuts, and beans.
- **Include lean proteins:** (meat from chicken, fish, or other lean sources). These foods provide building blocks for healthy muscles, skin, and bones. Also, eat a wide variety of foods. A varied diet provides the nutrients your body needs while preventing any known risk factors (such as heart disease) from occurring.
- **Limit sugar to no more than 10% of your total daily calories:** This limit means that you can eat foods like fruit, vegetables, and other carbohydrates (like potatoes and pasta). You can also include some protein in your meals if these foods have little or no carbohydrates.
- **Work out for 30 minutes or more per day:** If you live within walking distance of a park, the amount of time is even greater. The benefits are many: improved blood sugar control, weight loss, increased energy, and lower blood cholesterol levels.
- **Reduce the amount of alcohol you drink:** Drinking alcohol is a commonly implicated risk factor for diabetes. When alcohol is consumed, glucose levels go up because the liver must break down and store all the alcohol as fat. When this happens, insulin may be less effective at bringing glucose into the cells. This can lead to diabetes and heart disease over time.

- **Take aspirin to reduce your risk of heart disease:** The benefits are many: reduced blood cholesterol levels, less inflamed blood vessels, possibly fewer strokes, and even better memory. You should take one low-dose aspirin daily to reduce your risk of heart disease.
- **Get regular exercise:** Aerobic exercise like walking, swimming, and dancing is beneficial for everyone, but especially for people over 60 years old. There are many forms of aerobic exercise. Some are as simple as walking or stretching; others are more advanced. The American Diabetes Association suggests that you participate in an activity for a minimum of 20 minutes three times per week (on nonconsecutive days).
- **Get regular blood pressure checks:** High blood pressure can increase your risk of heart disease, stroke, and diabetes, and it may also cause blindness, kidney failure, nerve damage, and other health problems.
- **Stay away from tobacco:** Smoking can lead to diabetes and is linked with a host of other diseases. Tobacco smoke contains more than 4,000 chemicals, many of which are known to damage a person's health. The nicotine in tobacco also gets into saliva and causes your body to absorb the more harmful chemicals even more rapidly. If you smoke, quit. The best way is to smoke a cigarette that contains only nicotine and no tobacco (such as an electronic cigarette) for a period of at least two weeks.
- **Avoid heavy drinking:** Heavy drinking is defined as one drink per day for women and two drinks for men. If you do drink alcohol, limit yourself to only one drink maximum per day (for women) or two drinks max per day (for guys).
- **Learn your family history:** If your family has diabetes, consult with a doctor who can help you lower your own risk by offering advice about food, physical activity, and other factors that influence blood sugar levels and weight. If a parent or sibling has diabetes, it is important to talk with a doctor about whether genetic tests are recommended.
- It is advisable to visit the doctor every 6 months for a checkup and be aware of all the early symptoms of diabetes.

All in all, type 2 diabetes can be prevented by a balanced diet, regular exercise, weight loss, and avoiding heavy drinking.

What to Eat and What to Avoid

Foods to Eat

Vegetables

Fresh vegetables never cause harm to anyone. So, adding a meal full of vegetables is the best shot for all diabetic patients. But not all vegetables contain the same amount of macronutrients. Some vegetables contain a high amount of carbohydrates, so those are not suitable for a diabetic diet. We need to use vegetables that contain a low amount of carbohydrates.

- Cauliflower
- Spinach
- Tomatoes
- Broccoli
- Lemons
- Artichoke
- Garlic
- Asparagus
- Spring onions

- Onions
- Ginger, etc.

Meat

Meat is not on the red list for the diabetic diet. It is fine to have some meat every now and then for diabetic patients. However, certain meat types are better than others. For instance, red meat is not a preferable option for such patients. They should consume white meat more often whether it's seafood or poultry. Healthy options for meat are the following:

- All fish, i.e., salmon, halibut, trout, cod, sardine, etc.
- Scallops
- Mussels
- Shrimp
- Oysters, etc.

Fruits

Not all fruits are good for diabetes. To know if the fruit is suitable for this diet, it is important to note its sugar content. Some fruits contain a high amount of sugar in the form of sucrose and fructose, and those should be readily avoided. Here is the list of popularly used fruits that can be taken on the diabetic diet:

- Peaches
- Nectarines
- Avocados
- Apples
- Berries
- Grapefruit
- Kiwi Fruit
- Bananas
- Cherries
- Grapes
- Orange
- Pears
- Plums
- Strawberries

Nuts and Seeds

Nuts and seeds are perhaps the most enriched edibles, and they contain such a mix of macronutrients that can never harm anyone. So, diabetic patients can take nuts and seeds in their diet without any fear of a glucose spike.

- Pistachios
- Sunflower seeds
- Walnuts
- Peanuts
- Pecans
- Pumpkin seeds
- Almonds

- Sesame seeds, etc.

Grains

Diabetic patients should also be selective while choosing the right grains for their diet. The idea is to keep the amount of starch as minimum as possible. That is why you won't see any white rice on the list; rather it is replaced with more fibrous brown rice.

- Quinoa
- Oats
- Multigrain
- Whole grains
- Brown rice
- Millet
- Barley
- Sorghum
- Tapioca

Fats

Fat intake is the most debated topic as far as the diabetic diet is concerned as there are diets like ketogenic, which are loaded with fats and still proved effective for diabetic patients. The key is the absence of carbohydrates. In any other situation, fats are as harmful to diabetics as to any normal person. Switching to unsaturated fats is a better option.

- Sesame oil
- Olive oil
- Canola oil
- Grapeseed oil
- Other vegetable oils
- Fats extracted from plant sources

Diary

Any dairy product which directly or indirectly causes a glucose rise in the blood should not be taken on this diet. Other than those, all products are good to use. These items include the following:

- Skimmed milk
- Low-fat cheese
- Eggs
- Yogurt
- Trans fat-free margarine or butter

Sugar Alternatives

Since ordinary sugars or sweeteners are strictly forbidden on a diabetic diet, there are artificial varieties that can add sweetness without raising the level of carbohydrates in the meal. These substitutes are the following:

- Stevia
- Xylitol
- Natvia
- Swerve

- Monk fruit
- Erythritol

Make sure to substitute them with extra care. The sweetness of each sweetener is entirely different from the table sugar, so add each in accordance with the intensity of their flavor. Stevia is the sweetest of them, and it should be used with more care. In place of 1 cup of sugar, a teaspoon of stevia is enough. All other sweeteners are more or less similar to sugar in their intensity of sweetness.

Foods to Avoid

Knowing a general scheme of diet helps a lot, but it is equally important to be well familiar with the items which have to be avoided. With this list, you can make your diet a hundred% sugar-free. There are many other food items that can cause some harm to a diabetic patient, as the sugars do. So, let's discuss them in some detail here.

Sugars

Sugar is a big NO-GO for a diabetic diet. Once you are diabetic, you would need to say goodbye to all the natural sweeteners that are loaded with carbohydrates. They contain polysaccharides, which readily break into glucose after getting into our bodies. And the list does not only include table sugars but other items like honey and molasses should also be avoided.

- White sugar
- Brown sugar
- Confectionary sugar
- Honey
- Molasses
- Granulated sugar

Your mind and your body will not accept the abrupt change. It is recommended to go for a gradual change. It means start substituting it with low-carb substitutes in small amounts, day by day.

High-Fat Dairy Products

Once you have diabetes, you may get susceptible to a number of other fatal diseases, including cardiovascular ones. That is why experts strictly recommend avoiding high-fat food products, especially dairy items. The high amount of fat can make your body insulin resistant. So, even when you take insulin, it won't be of any use as the body will not work on it.

Saturated Animal Fats

Saturated animal fats are not good for anyone, whether diabetic or normal. So, better avoid using them in general. Whenever you are cooking meat, try to trim off all the excess fat. Cooking oils made out of these saturated fats should be avoided. Keep yourself away from any animal-origin fats.

High Carb Vegetables

As discussed above, vegetables with more starch are not suitable for diabetes. These veggies can increase the carbohydrate levels of food. So, omit these from the recipes and enjoy the rest of the less starchy vegetables. Some of the high-carb vegetables are the following:

- Potatoes
- Sweet potatoes
- Yams, etc.

Cholesterol Rich Ingredients

Bad cholesterol or high-density lipoprotein has the tendency to deposit in different parts of the body. That is why food items having high bad cholesterol are not good for diabetes. Such items should be replaced with the ones with low cholesterol.

High Sodium Products

Sodium is related to hypertension and blood pressure. Since diabetes is already the result of a hormonal imbalance in the body, in the presence of excess sodium—another imbalance—a fluid imbalance may occur, which a diabetic body cannot tolerate. It adds up to already present complications of the disease. So, avoid using food items with a high amount of sodium. Mainly store packed items, processed foods, and salt all contain sodium, and one should avoid them all. Use only the "Unsalted" variety of food products, whether it's butter, margarine, nuts, or other items.

Sugary Drinks

Cola drinks or other similar beverages are filled with sugars. If you had seen different video presentations showing the amount of sugars present in a single bottle of soda, you would know how dangerous those are for diabetic patients. They can drastically increase the amount of blood glucose levels within 30 minutes of drinking. Fortunately, there are many sugar-free varieties available in the drinks, which are suitable for diabetic patients.

Sugar Syrups and Toppings

A number of syrups available in the markets are made out of nothing but sugar. Maple syrup is one good example. For a diabetic diet, the patient should avoid such sugary syrups and also stay away from the sugar-rich toppings available in the stores. If you want to use them at all, trust yourself and prepare them at home with a sugar-free recipe.

Sweet Chocolate and Candies

For diabetic patients, sugar-free chocolates or candies are the best way out. Other processed chocolate bars and candies are extremely damaging to their health, and all of these should be avoided. You can try and prepare healthy bars and candies at home with sugar-free recipes.

Alcohol

Alcohol has the tendency to reduce the rate of our metabolism and take away our appetite, which can render a diabetic patient into a very life-threatening condition. Alcohol in a very small amount cannot harm the patient, but regular or constant intake of alcohol is bad for health and glucose levels.

Treatment for Diabetes

The Importance of Insulin

Diabetes is a serious condition caused by a deficiency of insulin. Insulin is a hormone that is necessary for the proper functioning of the body. When a person develops diabetes, the cells in the body do not respond to insulin properly. The result is that the cells do not get the energy and nutrients they need, and then they start to die. Diabetes treatments differ depending on the kind, number, and severity of complications as well as the patient's overall health. Fortunately, diabetes has been studied extensively by the medical community, and as a result, there are numerous resources and treatments accessible.

For type 1 diabetes, insulin supplements are essential. Type 1 diabetics rely on daily insulin injections; some prefer a costlier but easier-to-use insulin pump. Insulin needs in type 1 diabetics will vary throughout the day as they eat and exercise. This means many type 1 diabetics will regularly test their blood sugar levels to assess whether their insulin needs are being met. Some type 1 diabetics develop insulin resistance after years of injections. This means that oral diabetes medication such as metformin is becoming increasingly more commonly prescribed to type 1 diabetic individual to help prevent insulin resistance.

In some circumstances, type 2 diabetes can be managed without the need for medication. Many type 2 diabetic individuals can control their blood sugar levels by watching what they eat and doing some modest exercise. The majority of type 2 diabetics are advised to stick to low-fat, high-fiber, and low-carbohydrate diets. Medication is required for some persons with type 2 diabetes. Type 2 diabetes, unlike type 1, does not demand the use of insulin as frequently. Some type 2 diabetics, however, require insulin to complement their pancreas production.

Metformin is the most widely given type 2 diabetic medication. This prescription medication aids in the reduction of blood glucose levels and the improvement of insulin sensitivity. Other drugs prescribed to type 2 diabetics include sulfonylureas, thiazolidinediones, and meglitinides, which all help increase insulin production or sensitivity.

Chapter 2. What Is an Air Fryer?

The air fryer has become the most popular and trendy kitchen appliance this year. But why are people excited about it? Why has it become a favorite of people who love fried food? Why is it promoting frying being healthy? The air fryer is nothing like a typical deep fryer. This cooking utensil is much more like a small, stylish, and self-contained oven that uses a convection cooking method. It uses an electrical element that heats the air in the fryer and then circulates it evenly around the food for its cooking. As a result, this hot air cooks the food in the fryer quickly and brings out well-cooked food that is evenly browned and crunchy on the outside, but the inside stays moist and tasty.

Advantages of Using an Air Fryer

- **Healthier cooking:** With an air fryer, frying your food is healthy. How? The air fryer only needs just a tiny sprit of oil or no oil at all to cook. You can easily cook fries, chicken wings, onion rings, and much more and still get crispy foods without the extra oil. And, compared to oven and deep-frying cooking, the foods from the air fryer, especially fries, are crispier and not dried out, making the food even more impressive.
- **Quicker meals:** Since the air fryer is smaller than the oven, it circulates hot air around its fan quickly, which cooks the food faster. The air fryer needs only a small amount of time to reach the cooking temperature compared to an oven, which may take 20 minutes or more to properly preheat and begin cooking. So, if you need to make your meals in a hurry, you will love the air fryer's time-saving features.
- **Versatility:** The air fryer doesn't only just do frying; you can do so much more cooking with it! The air fryer can also roast, grill, stir-fry, broil, and even bakes cakes. You can make fresh or frozen food in it, or reheat the leftovers. Make use of an air fryer and additional accessories like a cake pan, pizza pan, rotisserie rack, frill pan, and steamer inserts to cook a variety of foods.
- **Space saver:** If you live in a dorm, share a house, or have a small kitchen, then you will definitely appreciate the small size of an air fryer. The air fryer comes in different sizes, but its small size can be of a coffee maker size, which won't take too much room on your kitchen counter. Hence, an air fryer is easy to move or store away. The air fryer is also handy to take on your travel ventures and place in your office kitchen to cook fresh food.
- **Ease of clean-up:** Most cooks don't enjoy the cleanup of kitchen utensils, but with an air fryer, this won't be a trouble for you in any way. The air fryer just has a fryer basket and pan to clean, which is dishwasher safe and takes a few minutes to wash up after cooking. And, the cooking basket or pan is non-stick, so food usually doesn't stick to it and instead slides onto the plate easily.

How to Cook in an Air Fryer

Here's how you can start cooking with your air fryer and get the most out of it.

1. **Adjust the cooking temperature:** Although there are many air frying recipes at the beginning of your air fryer cooking, you should stick to them to understand how air fryer cooking works and proficient air frying cooking skills. Then, move on to convert your regular deep-frying or oven-baked recipes into air-frying ones. For this, reduce the cooking temperature by 25°F to achieve the same result in terms of texture and taste of your food. For example, if your recipe is deep-fried in the oil heated to 350°F, then air fryer the same food at 325°F. This rule applies to other converting recipes, be it baking, roasting, broiling, etc. Remember to pre-heat your air fryer to a temperature of 220°F or

the recipe suggested temperature; it usually takes 5 minutes, and then fill the frying basket for further cooking.

2. **Toss the ingredients with oil:** Although the cooking accessories of the air fryer are non-stick, still you should toss your food ingredients in oil, about 1 to 2 tablespoons. You can skip this step for foods that are naturally fatty like meatballs. And, for foods that are coated in flour or battered, cook them in the greased frying basket and then coat the top of the food with an oil spray. This oil is essential to make sure that air-fried food turns out golden brown, crunchy and appealing.

3. **Filling the frying basket:** Foods coated with flour or battered should be fried in one layer in the air fryer. For foods like fries or vegetables, you can load the frying basket to the top, but a full basket takes a long cooking time and may result in food that is not quite crispy. It is also recommended to shake the basket at least twice to make sure the food is cooked evenly.

4. **Check the doneness early:** The hot air circulation in the air fryer helps in maintaining a consistent temperature in the air fryer, which tends to cook the food faster than being cooked in a conventional oven and deep fryer. This means that if you are converting your regular food into an air-frying one or the recipe you have already cooked in an air fryer, you will need to check the food for about two-thirds of the suggested cooking time to test its doneness. For example, if the fish sticks recipe says to be cooked in 15 minutes, then start checking them at 10 minutes.

How to Use Your Air Fryer

1. **Prepare the ingredients:** To stop ingredients from adhering to the fry basket, ensure you grease it with cooking spray or one tablespoonful of cooking oil. Also, steer clear of stuffing the fry basket with too much food when cooking; else, many areas in the food will not cook correctly. When using wet ingredients or those immersed in fluids or marinated, ensure you dry them using paper towels, as this will help avert the splashing of fluids or the production of too much smoke as a result of the excess fluids.

2. **Setting the temperature and time:** Move on to convert your regular deep frying or oven-baked recipes into air frying ones.

3. **Check food during cooking:** When preparing small or frozen ingredients in the air fryer, it is important that you rattle it a number of times to ensure that the heat cooks the ingredients uniformly. Add water into the air fryer drawer to prevent excessive smoke and heat. Shake the basket or flip the food for even cooking at the halfway mark.

4. **Cleaning the air fryer:** After every use, make sure you clean your air fryer to avoid making the unit smoke. If you don't enjoy cleaning, you are in luck because air fryers are easy to clean. Use a paper towel to rub off the grate and drawer when it doesn't require thorough cleaning. You easily hand wash it if it is gunky. Check your product's manual to see if some parts of your air fryer are dishwasher safe.

5. **Prepare the air fryer:** Place the air fryer on a level and heatproof kitchen top. Prepare the food. Grease the basket with a little oil and add a bit more to the food to avoid sticking. If the food is marinated, pat it dry lightly to prevent splattering and excess smoke. Use aluminum foil for easy cleaning.

6. **Before cooking:** Preheat the air fryer for 3 minutes before cooking. Avoid overcrowding and leave sufficient space for air circulation.

7. **Using oil sprays:** Although the Air Fryer's cooking accessories are non-stick, you should still toss your food ingredients in oil, about 1 to 2 tablespoons. Oil is essential to make sure that air-fried food turns out golden brown, crunchy and appealing.

8. **Using the basket or rack:** Foods coated with flour or battered should be fried in one layer in the Air Fryer. For foods like fries or vegetables, you can load the frying basket to the top, but a full basket

takes a long cooking time and may result in food that is not quite crispy. It is also recommended to shake the basket at least twice to make sure the food is cooked evenly.

9. **Keep an eye on the timing:** The circulation in the Air Fryer helps in maintaining a consistent temperature, which cooks the food faster than being cooked in a conventional oven and deep fryer. This is worth it if you are adapting your regular food into an Air Fryer or the recipe you have already cooked in it, you will need to check the food about two-thirds of the suggested cooking time to test its doneness. For example, if the fish sticks recipe says to be cooked in 15 minutes, then start checking them at 10 minutes.

Why Should the Diabetic Use Air Fryer?

Many studies have pinpointed that fried foods are bad for health and well-being. But, the cooking method in an air fryer promotes a healthier way to fry food without compromising its taste and crunchiness. And this makes the air fryer good for health-conscious individuals and diabetics.

Here's why: The main reason for this claim is the use of less oil in cooking foods with an air fryer, and this cut up to 80% of the fat compared to the deep fryer. Isn't that huge?! And the fried foods in it have a similar taste and texture to regular deep-fried foods. Furthermore, studies have confirmed that consuming too many fried foods increases the risks of obesity in adults. The more you consume fried food, the more you will have the risk of developing diabetes. However, if you consume fried foods often, it can risk your health with type 2 diabetes. Thus, you should switch to air-fried cooking to lower the intake of fats and/or to lose weight without cutting down your fried food diet. Air fryer reduces the fat content, which would drastically reduce the number of calories by a significant amount. For example, deep-fried chicken wings are extremely fatty, but air-fried chicken wings contain less fat and more protein.

The fewer fats and calories with preserved nutrition and ingredients are good for health freaks, weight watchers, and diabetics. Foods that are deep-fried have more calories and fats compared to the ones that are prepared in the air fryer. And, these fats and calories are way too high to be part of a healthy diet. Thus, eating low-fat food prepared in an air fryer impacts your health positively. Thereby, it will reduce the risks of health conditions like:

- Obesity
- Heart diseases
- Heart attacked
- Blocked arteries
- Internal inflammation

With this information in mind, you can understand how the air fryer benefits anyone who is trying to control or prevent diabetes and eat healthier.

To receive your FREE eBook "The Anti-inflammatory Cookbook" Scan this QR Code

Chapter 3. Breakfast Recipes

1. Air Fryer Meatballs in Tomato Sauce

Preparation Time: 5 minutes

Cooking Time: 13 minutes

Servings: 4

Ingredients:

- 1 egg
- ¾ lb lean ground beef
- 1 onion, chopped
- 3 tbsp breadcrumbs
- ½ tbsp fresh thyme leaves, chopped
- ½ cup tomato sauce
- 1 tbsp parsley, chopped
- Pinch salt
- Pinch pepper, to taste

Directions:

1. Preheat Air Fryer to 390°F.
2. Place all ingredients in a bowl. Mix until well combined. Divide the mixture into 12 balls. Place in cooking basket.
3. Cook meatballs for 8 minutes.
4. Put cooked meatballs in an oven dish. Pour tomato sauce on top. Put the oven dish inside the cooking basket of the Air Fryer.
5. Cook for 5 minutes at 330°F.

Nutrition:

- **Calories:** 129
- **Carbohydrates:** 15.4 g
- **Fat:** 17.8 g
- **Protein:** 17.6 g

2. Chicken Fried Spring Rolls

Preparation Time: 6 minutes

Cooking Time: 28 minutes

Servings: 4

Ingredients:

For spring roll wrappers:

- 1 egg, beaten
- 8 spring roll wrappers
- 1 tsp cornstarch
- ½ tsp olive oil

For filling:

- 1 cup chicken breast, cooked, shredded
- 1 celery stalk, sliced thinly
- 1 carrot, sliced thinly
- 1 tsp chicken stock powder, low sodium
- ½ tsp ginger, chopped finely
- ½ cup sliced mushrooms

Directions:

1. Preheat Air Fryer to 390°F.
2. Prepare the filling. Combine shredded chicken, mushrooms, carrot, and celery in a bowl. Add in chicken stock powder, and ginger. Stir well.
3. Meanwhile, mix cornstarch and egg until thick in a bowl. Set aside.
4. Spoon some filling into a spring roll wrapper. Roll and seal the end with the egg mixture.
5. Lightly brush spring rolls with oil and place them in the cooking basket. Cook for 4 minutes. Serve.

Nutrition:

- **Calories:** 150
- **Carbohydrates:** 18 g

- **Fat:** 5 g
- **Protein:** 9 g

3. Air-Fried Cinnamon Biscuit Bite

Preparation Time: 25 minutes

Cooking Time: 16 minutes

Servings: 8

Ingredients:

- $^2/_3$ cup all-purpose flour
- $^2/_3$ cup whole-wheat flour
- ¼ tsp ground cinnamon
- ¼ tsp salt
- $^1/_3$ cup whole milk
- 1 tsp baking powder
- 4 tbsp cold salted butter
- Cooking spray
- 2 cups powdered sugar
- 3 tbsp water

Directions:

1. Cut cold salted butter into small pieces. Add salt, cinnamon, baking powder, and flour together in a bowl; whisk them together. Add butter to the mixture and stir it until the mixture is even.
2. Add milk to the mixture and stir it together until it forms dough balls. Knead dough on a surface that has some flour. Knead dough into smooth and cohesive balls. This should take half a minute.
3. Now, you can cut the dough into 16 pieces and gently roll each of them into a smooth ball.
4. Coat the air fryer basket with cooking spray. Then, you can cook the dough at 350°F until it puffs up and goes brown. Cooking should be for about 10 to 12 minutes.
5. Now, you can remove the doughnut balls and place them on a wire rack over a foil. Do the same with other dough balls.
6. To serve people who are not diabetic, you can mix some granulated sugar with water

and sprinkle the solution on doughnut balls.

Nutrition:

- **Calories:** 325
- **Carbohydrates:** 1 g
- **Protein:** 8 g
- **Fat:** 7 g

4. Macaroni Cheese Toast

Preparation Time: 5 minutes

Cooking Time: 8 minutes

Servings: 2

Ingredients:

- 1 beaten egg
- 4 tbsp cheddar cheese
- Salt and pepper
- ½ cup macaroni and cheese
- 4 bread slices

Directions:

1. Spread the cheese and macaroni and cheese over two bread slices.
2. Place other bread slices on top of the cheese and cut diagonally.
3. In a bowl, place the beaten egg and season with salt and pepper.
4. Brush some egg mixture onto the bread.
5. Place bread into the air fryer and cook at 300°F for 5 minutes.

Nutrition:

- **Calories:** 250
- **Carbohydrates:** 9 g
- **Fat:** 16 g
- **Protein:** 14 g

5. Mushroom and Cheese Frittata

Preparation Time: 7 minutes

Cooking Time: 20 minutes

Servings: 4

Ingredients:

- 6 eggs
- 6 cups button mushrooms, sliced thinly
- 1 red onion, sliced into thin rounds
- 6 tbsp feta cheese, reduced fat, crumbled
- Pinch of salt
- 2 tbsp olive oil

Directions:

1. Preheat Air Fryer to 330°F.
2. Sauté onions and mushrooms. Transfer to a plate with a paper towel.
3. Meanwhile, beat eggs in a bowl. Season with salt. Coat a baking dish with cooking spray. Pour egg mixture.
4. Add in mushrooms and onions. Top with crumbled feta cheese.
5. Place baking dish in Air fryer basket. Cook for 20 minutes. Serve.

Nutrition:

- **Calories:** 140
- **Carbohydrates:** 5.4 g
- **Fat:** 10.6 g
- **Protein:** 22.7 g

6. Air-Fried Flaxseed French Toast Sticks with Berries

Preparation Time: 21 minutes

Cooking Time: 40 minutes

Servings: 4

Ingredients:

- Cooking spray
- 8 tsp pure maple syrup, divided
- 4 whole-grain bread slices
- $2/3$ cup flaxseed meal
- 2 large eggs
- 2 cups of sliced fresh strawberries
- ¼ cup reduced-fat milk
- ½ tsp ground cinnamon
- 1 tsp vanilla extract

Directions:

6. Divide each slice of bread into 4 sticks. Mix cinnamon, vanilla, milk, and eggs in a small bowl.
7. Place flaxseed meal in another bowl. Soak pieces of bread in egg mixture, one piece at a time. Then, transfer sticks of bread soaked in a flaxseed meal for coating.
8. After that, you need to coat bread sticks with cooking spray.
9. Arrange breadsticks in your air fryer basket, but make sure there are spaces between them.
10. Cook them at 375°F for just 5 minutes. You can turn them over before you cook them for another 5 minutes. They should be crunchy and golden brown by then.
11. Place them on a plate and top sticks of bread with ½ cup strawberries and 2 tsp maple syrup, and serve them.

Nutrition:

- **Calories:** 361
- **Carbohydrates:** 5 g
- **Protein:** 14 g
- **Fat:** 10 g

7. Cinnamon and Cheese Pancake

Preparation Time: 5 minutes

Cooking Time: 10 minutes

Servings: 4

Ingredients:

- 2 eggs
- 2 cups cream cheese, reduced fat
- ½ tsp cinnamon
- 1 pack Stevia

Directions:

1. Preheat Air Fryer to 330°F.
2. Meanwhile, combine cream cheese, cinnamon, eggs, and Stevia in a blender.
3. Pour ¼ of the mixture in Air fryer basket. Cook for 2 minutes on each side. Repeat the process with the rest of the mixture. Serve.

Nutrition:

- **Calories:** 140
- **Carbohydrates:** 5.4 g
- **Fat:** 10.6 g
- **Protein:** 22.7 g

8. Low-Carb White Egg and Spinach Frittata

Preparation Time: 6 minutes

Cooking Time: 16 minutes

Servings: 4

Ingredients:

- 8 egg whites
- 2 cups fresh spinach
- 2 tbsp olive oil
- 1 green pepper, chopped
- 1 red pepper, chopped
- ½ cup feta cheese, reduced fat, crumbled
- ¼ of a yellow onion, chopped
- 1 tsp salt
- 1 tsp pepper

Directions:

1. Preheat Air Fryer to 330°F.
2. Place red and green peppers and onions in an Air Fryer basket and cook for 3 minutes. Season with salt and pepper.
3. Pour egg whites and cook for 4 minutes. Add spinach and feta cheese on top.
4. Cook for 5 minutes.
5. Transfer to a plate. Slice and serve.

Nutrition:

- **Calories:** 120
- **Carbohydrates:** 13 g
- **Fat:** 4.5 g
- **Protein:** 9.9 g

9. Scallion Sandwich

Preparation Time: 5 minutes

Cooking Time: 12 minutes

Servings: 1

Ingredients:

- 2 slices of wheat bread
- 2 tsp butter, low fat
- 2 scallions, sliced thinly
- 1 tbsp parmesan cheese, grated
- ¾ cup cheddar cheese, reduced fat, grated

Directions:

1. Preheat the Air fryer to 356°F.
2. Spread the butter on a slice of bread. Place inside the cooking basket with the butter side facing down.
3. Place cheese and scallions on top. Spread the rest of the butter on the other slices of bread. Put it on top of the sandwich and sprinkle it with parmesan cheese.
4. Cook for 10 minutes.

Nutrition:

- **Calories:** 154
- **Carbohydrates:** 9 g
- **Fat:** 2.5 g
- **Protein:** 8.6 g

10. Lean Lamb and Turkey Meatballs with Yogurt

Preparation Time: 11 minutes

Cooking Time: 13 minutes

Servings: 4

Ingredients:

- 1 egg white
- 4 oz ground lean turkey
- 1 lb ground lean lamb
- 1 tsp each of cayenne pepper, ground coriander, red chili paste, salt, and ground cumin
- 2 garlic cloves, minced
- 1 ½ tbsp parsley, chopped
- 1 tbsp mint, chopped
- ¼ cup olive oil

For yogurt:

- 2 tbsp buttermilk
- 1 garlic clove, minced
- ¼ cup mint, chopped

- ½ cup Greek yogurt, non-fat
- Salt to taste

Directions:

1. Set Air Fryer to 390°F.
2. Mix all ingredients for meatballs in a bowl. Roll and mold them into golf-size round pieces. Arrange in cooking basket. Cook for 8 minutes.
3. While waiting, combine all ingredients for mint yogurt in a bowl. Mix well.
4. Serve meatballs with mint yogurt. Top with olives and fresh mint.

Nutrition:

- **Calories:** 154
- **Carbohydrates:** 9 g
- **Fat:** 2.5 g
- **Protein:** 8.6 g

11.   Air Fried Eggs

Preparation Time: 9 minutes

Cooking Time: 18 minutes

Servings: 4

Ingredients:

- 4 eggs
- 2 cups baby spinach, rinsed
- 1 tbsp extra-virgin olive oil
- 8 slices of bacon
- ½ cup cheddar cheese, reduced-fat, shredded, divided
- Pinch of salt
- Pinch of pepper

Directions:

1. Preheat Air Fryer to 350°F.
2. Heat oil in a pan over a medium-high flame. Cook spinach until wilted. Drain excess liquid. Put cooked spinach into 4 greased ramekins.
3. Add a slice of bacon to each ramekin, crack an egg, and put cheese on top. Season with salt and pepper.
4. Put ramekins inside the cooking basket of the Air Fryer.

5. Cook for 15 minutes.

Nutrition:

- **Calories:** 106
- **Carbohydrates:** 10 g
- **Fat:** 3.2 g
- **Protein:** 9.0 g
- **1.** Lb. bacon

12.   Cinnamon Pancake

Preparation Time: 5 minutes

Cooking Time: 19 minutes

Servings: 4

Ingredients:

- 2 eggs
- 2 cups cream cheese, reduced fat
- ½ tsp cinnamon
- 1 pack Stevia

Directions:

1. Preheat Air Fryer to 330°F.
2. Combine cream cheese, cinnamon, eggs, and stevia in a blender.
3. Pour ¼ of the mixture in Air fryer basket.
4. Cook for 2 minutes on each side.
5. Repeat the process with the rest of the mixture. Serve.

Nutrition:

- **Calories:** 106
- **Carbohydrates:** 10 g
- **Fat:** 3.2 g
- **Protein:** 9.0 g

12.   Spinach and Mushrooms Omelet

Preparation Time: 11 minutes

Cooking Time: 18 minutes

Servings: 4

Ingredients:

- ½ cup spinach leaves
- 1 cup mushrooms

- 3 green onions
- 1 cup water
- ½ tsp turmeric
- ½ red bell pepper
- 2 tbsp butter, low fat
- 1 cup almond flour
- ½ tsp onion powder
- ½ tsp garlic powder
- ½ tsp fresh pepper
- ¼ tsp ground thyme
- 2 tbsp extra virgin olive oil
- 1 tsp black salt
- Salsa, store-bought

Directions:

1. Preheat Air Fryer to 300°F.
2. Rinse spinach leaves over tap water. Set aside.
3. In a mixing bowl, combine green onions, onion powder, garlic powder, red bell pepper, mushrooms, turmeric, thyme, olive oil, salt, and pepper. Mix well.
4. In another bowl, combine water and flour to form a smooth paste.
5. In a pan, heat the olive oil. Sauté peppers and mushrooms for 3 minutes. Tip in spinach and cook for 3 minutes. Set aside.
6. In the Air fryer basket, pour omelet batter. Cook for 3 minutes before flipping. Place vegetables on top. Season with salt. Serve with salsa on the side.

Nutrition:

- **Calories:** 110
- **Carbohydrates:** 9 g
- **Fat:** 1.3 g
- **Protein:** 5.4 g

13.   All Berries Pancakes

Preparation Time: 5 minutes

Cooking Time: 20 minutes

Servings: 4

Ingredients:

- ½ cup frozen blueberries, thawed
- ½ cup frozen cranberries, thawed

- 1 cup coconut milk
- 2 tbsp coconut oil, for greasing
- 2 tbsp stevia
- 1 cup whole wheat flour, finely milled
- 1 tbsp baking powder
- 1 tsp vanilla extract
- ¼ tsp salt

Directions:

1. Preheat Air Fryer to 330°F.
2. In a mixing bowl, combine coconut oil, coconut milk, flour, stevia, baking powder, vanilla extract, and salt.
3. Gently fold in berries. Divide batter into equal portions. Pour into the Air fryer basket. Flip once the edges are set. Do not press down on pancakes.
4. Transfer to a plate. Sprinkle palm sugar. Serve.

Nutrition:

- **Calories:** 57
- **Carbohydrates:** 14 g
- **Fat:** 0.3 g
- **Protein:** 0.7 g

14.   Air Fried Aubergine and Tomato

Preparation Time: 6 minutes

Cooking Time: 14 minutes

Servings: 2

Ingredients:

- 1 aubergine, sliced thickly into 4 disks
- 1 tomato, sliced into 2 thick disks
- 2 tsp feta cheese, reduced fat
- 2 fresh basil leaves, minced
- 2 balls, small buffalo mozzarella, reduced fat, roughly torn

Directions:

1. Preheat Air Fryer to 330°F.
2. Spray a small amount of oil into the Air fryer basket. Fry aubergine slices for 5 minutes or until golden brown on both sides. Transfer to a plate.

3. Fry tomato slices in batches for 5 minutes or until seared on both sides.
4. To serve, stack salad starting with an aubergine base, buffalo mozzarella, basil leaves, tomato slice, and ½ tsp feta cheese.
5. Top off with another slice of aubergine and ½ tsp feta cheese. Serve.

Nutrition:

- **Calories:** 140.3
- **Carbohydrates:** 26.6 g
- **Fat:** 3.4 g
- **Protein:** 4.2 g

15. Quick Fry Chicken with Cauliflower

Preparation Time: 5 minutes

Cooking Time: 18 minutes

Servings: 4

Ingredients:

For quick fry:

- 1½ lb chicken thigh fillets, diced
- 1 piece, small red bell pepper, julienned
- 1 piece, thumb-sized ginger, grated
- 2 tbsp olive oil
- 1 clove, large garlic, minced
- 2 stalks, large leeks, minced
- 1 can, 5 oz water chestnuts, quartered
- 1 head, small cauliflower, cut into bite-sized florets
- ¾ cups chicken stock, low sodium

Seasonings:

- 1 tsp stevia
- 1 tbsp fish sauce
- ½ tbsp cornstarch, dissolved in
- 4 tbsp water
- Pinch salt
- Pinch black pepper, to taste

Garnish:

- Leeks, minced
- 1 piece, large lime, cut into 6 wedges

Directions:

1. Preheat Air Fryer to 330°F.
2. Pour olive oil in a pan. Swirl pan to coat. Sauté garlic, ginger, and leeks for 2 minutes. Set aside. Add in water chestnuts, cauliflower, red bell pepper, and chicken broth. Stir well. Cook for 15 minutes.
3. Meanwhile, put the chicken in the Air fryer basket. Fry until seared and golden brown.
4. Add seasoning to the pan. Stir and cook until the juice thickens.
5. Ladle 1 portion of quick fry veggies and chicken. Garnish with leeks and lemon wedges on the side. Serve.

Nutrition:

- **Calories:** 220
- **Carbohydrates:** 13.6 g
- **Fat:** 9 g
- **Protein:** 30.5 g

16. Air Fried Artichoke Hearts

Preparation Time: 5 minutes

Cooking Time: 8 minutes

Servings: 3

Ingredients:

- 1 lb frozen artichoke hearts, thawed, quartered
- 1 cup plain yogurt, low fat
- 2 eggs, whisked
- 1 cup almond flour, finely milled
- 1 cup almond flour, coarsely milled
- 1 small lime, sliced into wedges, pips removed
- ½ cup sour cream, reduced fat
- Pinch of salt

Directions:

1. Preheat Air Fryer to 330°F.
2. In a bowl, combine yogurt and salt. Soak artichoke hearts for 15 minutes. Drain. Discard yogurt.

3. Dredge artichokes in almond flour first, then into eggs, and into coarse-milled almond flour.
4. Layer artichoke hearts into the Air Fryer basket. Fry for 5 minutes or until golden brown on all sides. Drain on paper towels. Squeeze lime juice. Serve with lime wedges and sour cream on the side.

Nutrition:

- **Calories:** 67
- **Carbohydrates:** 7 g
- **Fat:** 3 g
- **Protein:** 2 g

17. Air-Fryer Onion Strings

Preparation Time: 15 minutes

Cooking Time: 8 minutes

Servings: 4

Ingredients:

- 2 cups buttermilk
- 1 piece whole white onion, halved, julienned
- 2 cups almond flour, finely milled
- ½ tsp cayenne pepper
- Pinch of salt
- Pinch of black pepper to taste

Directions:

1. Preheat Air Fryer to 330°F.
2. Soak onion strings in buttermilk for 1 hour before frying. Drain.
3. Meanwhile, mix almond flour, cayenne pepper, salt, and pepper in a bowl. Coat onion strings with flour mixture.
4. Layer onions in the Air fryer basket. Fry until golden brown and crisp. Drain on paper towels. Season with salt. Serve.

Nutrition:

- **Calories:** 150
- **Carbohydrates:** 13 g
- **Fat:** 17 g
- **Protein:** 2 g

18. Fried Spinach

Preparation Time: 14 minutes

Cooking Time: 11 minutes

Servings: 3

Ingredients:

- 2 ½ lb fresh spinach leaves and tender stems only
- Pinch of sea salt, to taste

Directions:

1. Preheat Air Fryer to 330°F.
2. Put spinach in the Air fryer basket. Fry for 20 seconds. Drain on paper towels. Repeat the step with the rest of the spinach. Season with salt. Serve.

Nutrition:

- **Calories:** 81.6
- **Carbohydrates:** 4.5 g
- **Fat:** 6.9 g
- **Protein:** 1.3 g

19. Air Fried Zucchini Flowers

Preparation Time: 14 minutes

Cooking Time: 12 minutes

Servings: 3

Ingredients:

- 2 ½ lb zucchini flowers, rinsed
- 1 cup almond flour, finely milled
- Pinch of sea salt, to taste
- Balsamic vinegar, for garnish
- Oil

Directions:

1. Preheat Air Fryer to 330°F.
2. Half-fill deep fryer with oil. Set this at medium heat. Lightly season zucchini flowers with salt, and then dredge in almond flour.
3. Layer breaded flowers into the Air Fryer basket. Fry until golden brown. Drain on

paper towels. Transfer to a plate. Pour balsamic vinegar if using. Serve.

Nutrition:

- **Calories:** 117
- **Carbohydrates:** 8 g
- **Fat:** 8 g
- **Protein:** 1 g

20. Garlic Bread with Cheese Dip

Preparation Time: 8 minutes

Cooking Time: 16 minutes

Servings: 8

Ingredients:

Fried garlic bread:

- 1 medium baguette, halved lengthwise, cut sides toasted
- 2 garlic cloves, whole
- 4 tbsp extra virgin olive oil
- 2 tbsp fresh parsley, minced

Blue cheese dip:

- 1 tbsp fresh parsley, minced
- ¼ cup fresh chives, minced
- ¼ tsp tabasco sauce
- 1 tbsp lemon juice, freshly squeezed
- ½ cup Greek yogurt, low fat
- ¼ cup blue cheese, reduced fat
- $1/16$ tsp salt
- $1/16$ tsp white pepper

Directions:

1. Preheat the machine to 400°F.
2. Combine oil and parsley in a small bowl.
3. Vigorously rub garlic cloves on the cut/toasted sides of the baguette. Dispose of garlic nubs.
4. Using a pastry brush, spread parsley-infused oil on the cut side of the bread.
5. Place bread cut-side down on a chopping board. Slice into inch-thick half-moons.
6. Place bread slices in the Air Fryer basket. Fry for 3 to 5 minutes or until bread browns

a little. Shake the contents of the basket once midway through. Place cooked pieces on a serving platter. Repeat step for the remaining bread.

7. To prepare blue cheese dip, mix ingredients in a bowl.
8. Place equal portions of fried bread on plates. Serve with blue cheese dip on the side.

Nutrition:

- **Calories:** 209
- **Carbohydrates:** 29 g
- **Fat:** 8 g
- **Protein:** 2.9 g

21. Fried Mixed Veggies with Avocado Dip

Preparation Time: 9 minutes

Cooking Time: 11 minutes

Servings: 4

Ingredients:

- Oil, for spraying

Avocado-feta dip:

- 1 avocado, pitted, peeled, flesh scooped out
- 4 oz feta cheese, reduced fat
- 2 leeks, minced
- 1 lime, freshly squeezed
- ¼ cup fresh parsley, chopped roughly
- $1/16$ tsp black pepper
- $1/16$ tsp salt

Vegetables:

- 1 zucchini, sliced into matchsticks
- 1 carrot, sliced into matchsticks
- 1 cup panko breadcrumbs, add more if needed
- 1 parsnip, sliced into matchsticks
- 1 large egg, whisked, add more if needed
- 1 cup all-purpose flour, add more if needed
- $1/8$ tsp flaky salt

Directions:

1. Preheat Air Fryer to 400°F.
2. Season carrots, parsnips, and zucchini with salt.
3. Dredge carrots into flour first, then egg, and finally into breadcrumbs. Place breaded pieces on a baking sheet lined with parchment paper. Repeat the step for all carrots. Then do the same for parsnips and zucchini.
4. Lightly spray vegetables with oil. Place a generous handful of carrots in the Air Fryer basket. Fry for 10 minutes or until breading turns golden brown, shaking the contents of the basket once midway. Place cooked pieces on a plate. Repeat the step for the remaining carrots.
5. Do the earlier step for parsnips, and then zucchini.
6. For the dip, except for salt, place the remaining ingredients in a food processor. Pulse a couple of times, and then process to desired consistency scraping down sides of the machine often. Taste. Add salt only if needed. Place in an airtight container. Chill until needed.
7. Place equal portions of cooked vegetables on plates. Serve with a small amount of avocado-feta dip on the side.

Nutrition:

- **Calories:** 109
- **Carbohydrates:** 4.0 g
- **Fat:** 2.6 g
- **Protein:** 2.9 g

22. Sweet Potato Crisps

Preparation Time: 5 minutes

Cooking Time: 22 minutes

Servings: 8

Ingredients:

- 2 large sweet potatoes, shaved thin using a mandolin
- Spanish paprika and salt to taste
- Oil
- Sea salt, to taste

Dips, optional:

- ¼ cup cashew cheese
- ¼ cup spinach walnut pesto

Directions:

1. Preheat Air Fryer to 330°F.
2. Place sweet potatoes flat on baking sheets with spaces in between pieces. Drizzle in oil; season lightly with paprika and sea salt.
3. Put baking sheet inside Air fryer basket. Fry for 30 minutes. Cool completely to room temperature before serving. Serve with cashew cheese and spinach walnut pesto.

Nutrition:

- **Calories:** 122
- **Carbohydrates:** 15 g
- **Fat:** 6 g
- **Protein:** 1 g

23. Fried Green Tomatoes

Preparation Time: 8 minutes

Cooking Time: 22 minutes

Servings: 2

Ingredients:

- 2 green tomatoes, sliced into ¼ inch thick
- 1 cup buttermilk
- 1 cup panko bread crumbs
- ½ cup almond flour
- 1 tsp salt
- ½ tbsp Creole seasoning
- ½ tsp pepper

Directions:

1. Slice tomatoes to ¼-inch thickness. Sprinkle both sides with salt and pepper.
2. Put buttermilk, flour, and a mixture of panko crumbs and Creole seasoning in 3 different shallow containers. Dredge each slice of tomato in flour.
3. Dip it into buttermilk and coat with panko mixture. Gently press the coating to make them stick.

4. Put a rack in the cooking basket of the Air Fryer. Arrange 3 coated tomato slices on top of the rack and spray with non-stick cooking spray. Set the fryer to 400°F and cook for 5 minutes. Transfer cooked tomatoes to a platter and cook the rest of coated tomato slices.

5. Sprinkle cooked tomatoes with a little creole seasoning and serve them with ranch dressing.

Nutrition:

- **Calories:** 60
- **Carbohydrates:** 5 g
- **Fat:** 3.2 g
- **Protein:** 3.6 g

24.   Mushroom Frittata

Preparation Time: 7 minutes

Cooking Time: 26 minutes

Servings: 4

Ingredients:

- 2 eggs
- ½ cup fresh mushrooms, sliced
- 1 tbsp olive oil
- 1 Roma tomato, halved
- Pinch of salt
- Pinch of pepper

Directions:

1. Set Air Fryer to 400°F.
2. Sautee mushrooms until cooked through. Season mushrooms with salt and pepper to taste. Once cooked, transfer to a plate and set aside.
3. Cook tomato. Tomatoes will become tender when ready. Sprinkle salt and pepper on the tomatoes. Transfer them to a plate once they are cooked.
4. Cook eggs the way you prefer. For an English breakfast, eggs are usually either fried or scrambled.
5. Arrange mushrooms, the tomato and eggs on your plate. Serve.

Nutrition:

- **Calories:** 129
- **Carbohydrates:** 15.4 g
- **Fat:** 17.8 g
- **Protein:** 17.6 g

25.   Avocado Taco Fry

Preparation Time: 6 minutes

Cooking Time: 28 minutes

Servings: 4

Ingredients:

- 1 avocado
- 1 egg
- ½ cup panko breadcrumbs
- Salt, to taste
- Tortillas and toppings

Directions:

1. Remove flesh from each avocado shell and slice them into wedges.
2. Beat egg in a shallow bowl and put breadcrumbs in another bowl. Dip avocado into the bowl with beaten egg and coat with breadcrumbs. Sprinkle the coated wedges with a bit of salt.
3. Arrange them in a cooking basket in a single layer.
4. Set Air Fryer to 392°F and cook for 15 minutes. Shake the basket halfway through the cooking process.
5. Put them on tortillas with your preferred toppings.

Nutrition:

- **Calories:** 140
- **Carbohydrates:** 12 g
- **Fat:** 8.8 g
- **Protein:** 6 g

26.   Blueberry Cream Cheese Sandwich

Preparation Time: 9 minutes

Cooking Time: 21 minutes

Servings: 4

Ingredients:

- 4 slices of wheat bread
- ¼ cup fresh blueberries
- 1 ½ cups cornflakes, crumbled
- 4 tbsp whipped cream cheese, berry-flavored
- 2 eggs, beaten
- 2 tsp Stevia
- 1/3 cup milk, low fat
- ¼ tsp salt
- ¼ tsp ground nutmeg

Directions:

1. Preheat Air Fryer to 400°F.
2. Put eggs, salt, sugar, nutmeg, and milk in a bowl. Mix well.
3. In another bowl, mix whipped cream cheese and blueberries.
4. Slit the top part of the crust of each bread slice. Fill each slice with 2 tbsp berry mixture. Soak stuffed bread slices in egg mixture until completely covered.
5. Coat them with cornflakes and press to make them stick. Put coated bread slices in the cooking basket of the Air Fryer. Cook for 8 minutes.
6. Serve while hot.

Nutrition:

- **Calories:** 70
- **Carbohydrates:** 6 g
- **Fat:** 4.5 g
- **Protein:** 2 g

27. Tomatoes and Cheese Frittata

Preparation Time: 7 minutes

Cooking Time: 23 minutes

Servings: 4

Ingredients:

- 8 eggs
- 2 tomatoes
- ½ cup cheddar cheese, reduced fat
- 2 leeks, sliced
- 1 tbsp fresh thyme
- Pinch of salt
- Pinch of pepper
- Olive oil

Directions:

1. Preheat Air Fryer to 330°F.
2. In a baking dish, grease leeks with olive oil. Add eggs, cheese, salt, and pepper. Layer tomato slices on top.
3. Place baking dish onside Air fryer basket. Cook for 10 minutes.
4. Remove and transfer the frittata to a plate. Sprinkle with thyme. Serve.

Nutrition:

- **Calories:** 186
- **Carbohydrates:** 9.1 g
- **Fat:** 11.1 g
- **Protein:** 11.9 g

28. Egg White and Flax Crepes

Preparation Time: 8 minutes

Cooking Time: 26 minutes

Servings: 3

Ingredients:

- 3 egg whites only
- 2 tbsp ground flaxseed
- 2 eggs
- ¼ cup coconut flour
- ¼ cup almond milk
- ½ tbsp baking soda

Directions:

1. Get a large non-stick skillet hot over medium-high heat. Coat with cooking spray.
2. Combine all ingredients in a food processor or blender and blend until thoroughly combined.
3. Pour batter into the air fryer hot skillet and swirl around to create a large, thin circle.

4. Let cook until bubbles in batter begin to pop, gently easing up sides every few moments, about 3 minutes or less.
5. Flip crepes and cook on the other side until firm. Serve.

Nutrition:

- **Calories:** 78.7
- **Carbohydrates:** 5.5 g
- **Fat:** 5.3 g
- **Protein:** 3.1 g

29.   Bell Pepper, Salsa, and Taco Frittata

Preparation Time: 11 minutes

Cooking Time: 24 minutes

Servings: 4

Ingredients:

- 6 eggs
- ¾ cup cheddar cheese, reduced fat
- ¼ cup onions, chopped
- ¼ cup green bell peppers, chopped
- 1 cup salsa
- 2 tbsp taco seasoning
- 1 cup sour cream, low fat
- 1 oz milk, low fat
- Pinch of salt
- Pinch of pepper

Directions:

1. Preheat USA Air Fryer to 330°F.
2. Combine eggs, green bell pepper, taco seasoning, onions, milk, cheddar cheese, salt, and pepper in a bowl.
3. Transfer the mixture to a baking dish. Lightly grease with cooking spray. Put baking dish inside Air Fryer basket. Cook for 20 minutes.
4. Top with salsa and sour cream. Serve.

Nutrition:

- **Calories:** 140
- **Carbohydrates:** 5.3 g
- **Fat:** 17 g
- **Protein:** 17.6 g

Chapter 4. Sides and Vegetables Recipes

30. Ravioli

Preparation Time: 5 minutes

Cooking Time: 16 minutes

Servings: 4

Ingredients:

- 8 oz frozen vegan ravioli, thawed
- 1 tsp dried basil
- 1 tsp garlic powder
- $^1/_8$ tsp pepper
- ¼ tsp salt
- 1 tsp dried oregano
- 2 tsp nutritional yeast flakes
- ½ cup marinara sauce, unsweetened
- ½ cup panko breadcrumbs
- ¼ cup liquid from chickpeas can

Directions:

1. Place breadcrumbs in a bowl, sprinkle with salt, basil, oregano, and black pepper, add garlic powder and yeast and stir until mixed.
2. Take a bowl and then pour chickpeas liquid into it.

3. Working on one ravioli at a time, first dip a ravioli in chickpeas liquid and then coat it with a breadcrumbs mixture.
4. Prepare the remaining ravioli in the same manner, then take a fryer basket, grease it well with oil, and place the ravioli in it in a single layer.
5. Switch on the air fryer, insert the fryer basket, sprinkle oil on the ravioli, shut with its lid, set the fryer at 390°F, then cook for 6 minutes, turn the ravioli, and continue cooking for 2 minutes until nicely golden and heated thoroughly.
6. Cook the remaining ravioli in the same manner and serve with marinara sauce.

Nutrition:

- **Calories:** 150
- **Carbohydrates:** 27 g
- **Fat:** 3 g
- **Protein:** 2 g

31. Onion Rings

Preparation Time: 10 minutes

Cooking Time: 32 minutes

Servings: 4

Ingredients:

- 1 large white onion, peeled
- $^2/_3$ cup pork rinds
- 3 tbsp almond flour
- ½ tsp garlic powder
- ½ tsp paprika
- ¼ tsp salt
- 3 tbsp coconut flour
- 2 eggs, pastured
- Olive oil

Directions:

1. Switch on the air fryer, insert the fryer basket, grease it with olive oil, then shut its lid, set the fryer at 400°F and preheat for 10 minutes.

2. Meanwhile, slice the peeled onion into ½-inch thick rings.
3. Take a shallow dish, add almond flour and stir in garlic powder, paprika, and pork rinds; take another shallow dish, add coconut flour and salt and stir until mixed.
4. Crack eggs in a bowl and then whisk until combined.
5. Working on one onion ring at a time, first coat the onion rings in coconut flour mixture, then it in egg, and coat with pork rind mixture by scooping over the onion until evenly coated.
6. Open the fryer, place coated onion rings in it in a single layer, spray oil over onion rings, close with its lid and cook for 16 minutes until nicely golden and thoroughly cooked, flipping onion rings halfway through frying.
7. When the air fryer beeps, open its lid, transfer the onion rings onto a serving plate and cook the remaining onion rings in the same manner.
8. Serve straight away.

Nutrition:

- **Calories:** 135
- **Carbohydrates:** 8 g
- **Fat:** 7 g
- **Protein:** 8 g

32.   Cauliflower Fritters

Preparation Time: 10 minutes

Cooking Time: 14 minutes

Servings: 2

Ingredients:

- 5 cups chopped cauliflower florets
- ½ cup almond flour
- ½ tsp baking powder
- ½ tsp pepper
- ½ tsp salt
- 2 eggs, pastured

Directions:

1. Add chopped cauliflower to a blender or food processor, pulse until minced, and then tip the mixture into a bowl.
2. Add the remaining ingredients, stir well, and then shape the mixture into $1/_3$-inch patties, an ice cream scoop of mixture per patty.
3. Switch on the air fryer, insert the fryer basket, grease it with olive oil, then shut its lid, set the fryer at 390°F and preheat for 5 minutes.
4. Open the fryer, add cauliflower patties in it a single layer, spray oil over the patties, close with its lid and cook for 14 minutes at 375°F until nicely golden and cooked, flipping the patties halfway through frying.
5. Serve straight away with dip.

Nutrition:

- **Calories:** 272
- **Carbohydrates:** 57 g
- **Fat:** 0.3 g
- **Protein:** 11 g

33.   Zucchini Fritters

Preparation Time: 20 minutes

Cooking Time: 12 minutes

Servings: 4

Ingredients:

- 2 medium zucchinis, ends trimmed
- 3 tbsp almond flour
- 1 tbsp salt
- 1 tsp garlic powder
- ¼ tsp paprika
- ¼ tsp pepper
- ¼ tsp onion powder
- 1 egg, pastured

Directions:

1. Wash and pat dry zucchini, then cut its ends and grate zucchini.
2. Place grated zucchini in a colander, sprinkle with salt and let it rest for 10 minutes.

3. Then wrap the zucchini in a kitchen cloth, squeeze moisture from it as much as possible, and place the dried zucchini in another bowl.
4. Add remaining ingredients into zucchini and then stir until mixed.
5. Take the fryer basket, line it with parchment paper, grease it with oil and drop the zucchini mixture on it by a spoonful, about 1-inch apart and then spray well with oil.
6. Switch on the air fryer, insert the fryer basket, then shut its lid, set the fryer at 360°F, and cook the fritter for 12 minutes until nicely golden and cooked, flipping fritters halfway through frying.
7. Serve straight away.

Nutrition:

- **Calories:** 57
- **Carbohydrates:** 8 g
- **Fat:** 1 g
- **Protein:** 3 g

34.   Kale Chips

Preparation Time: 5 minutes

Cooking Time: 7 minutes

Servings: 2

Ingredients:

- 1 large bunch of kale
- ¾ tsp red chili powder
- 1 tsp salt
- ¾ tsp pepper

Directions:

1. Remove hard spines from kale leaves, then cut kale into small pieces and place them in a fryer basket.
2. Spray oil over kale, then sprinkle with salt, chili powder, and black pepper and toss until well mixed.
3. Switch on the air fryer, insert the fryer basket, then shut its lid, set the fryer at 375°F, and cook for 7 minutes until kale is crispy, shaking halfway through frying.

4. When the air fryer beeps, open its lid, transfer kale chips onto a serving plate and serve.

Nutrition:

- **Calories:** 66.2
- **Carbohydrates:** 7.3 g
- **Fat:** 4 g
- **Protein:** 2.5 g

35.   Radish Chips

Preparation Time: 5 minutes

Cooking Time: 20 minutes

Servings: 2

Ingredients:

- 8 oz radish slices
- ½ tsp garlic powder
- 1 tsp salt
- ½ tsp onion powder
- ½ tsp pepper

Directions:

1. Wash radish slices, pat them dry, place them in a fryer basket, and then spray oil on them until well coated.
2. Sprinkle salt, garlic powder, onion powder, and black pepper over radish slices, and then toss until well coated.
3. Switch on the air fryer, insert the fryer basket, then shut its lid, set the fryer at 370°F, and cook for 10 minutes, stirring slices halfway through.
4. Then spray oil on radish slices, shake the basket and continue frying for 10 minutes, stirring chips halfway through.
5. Serve straight away.

Nutrition:

- **Calories:** 21
- **Carbohydrates:** 1 g
- **Fat:** 1.8 g
- **Protein:** 0.2 g

36.   Zucchini Fries

Preparation Time: 10 minutes

Cooking Time: 20 minutes

Servings: 4

Ingredients:

- 2 medium zucchinis
- ½ cup almond flour
- ⅛ tsp pepper
- ½ tsp garlic powder
- ⅛ tsp salt
- 1 tsp Italian seasoning
- ½ cup grated parmesan cheese, reduced-fat
- 1 egg, pastured, beaten
- Olive oil

Directions:

1. Switch on the air fryer, insert the fryer basket, grease it with olive oil, then shut its lid, set the fryer at 400°F and preheat for 10 minutes.
2. Meanwhile, cut each zucchini in half and then cut each zucchini half into 4-inch-long pieces, each about ½-inch thick.
3. Place flour in a shallow dish, add the remaining ingredients except for the egg and stir until mixed.
4. Crack the egg in a bowl and then whisk until blended.
5. Working on one zucchini piece at a time, first dip it in egg, then coat it in almond flour mixture and place it on a wire rack.
6. Open the fryer, add zucchini pieces to it a single layer, spray oil over the zucchini, close with its lid and cook for 10 minutes until nicely golden and crispy, shaking halfway through frying.
7. Cook the remaining zucchini pieces in the same manner and serve.

Nutrition:

- **Calories:** 147
- **Carbohydrates:** 6 g
- **Fat:** 10 g
- **Protein:** 9 g

37.   Avocado Fries

Preparation Time: 10 minutes

Cooking Time: 20 minutes

Servings: 2

Ingredients:

- 1 medium avocado, pitted
- 1 egg
- ½ cup almond flour
- ¼ tsp salt
- ¼ tsp pepper
- Olive oil

Directions:

1. Switch on the air fryer, insert the fryer basket, grease it with olive oil, then shut its lid, set the fryer at 400°F and preheat for 10 minutes.
2. Meanwhile, cut the avocado in half and then cut each half into wedges, each about ½-inch thick.
3. Place flour in a shallow dish, add salt and black pepper and stir until mixed.
4. Crack the egg in a bowl and then whisk until blended.
5. Working on one avocado piece at a time, first dip it in egg, then coat it in almond flour mixture and place it on a wire rack.
6. Open the fryer, add avocado pieces in it in a single layer, spray oil over the avocado, close with its lid and cook for 10 minutes until nicely golden and crispy, shaking halfway through frying.
7. When the air fryer beeps, open its lid, transfer avocado fries onto a serving plate and serve.

Nutrition:

- **Calories:** 251
- **Carbohydrates:** 19 g
- **Fat:** 17 g
- **Protein:** 6 g

38. Roasted Peanut Butter Squash

Preparation Time: 5 minutes

Cooking Time: 22 minutes

Servings: 4

Ingredients:

- 1 butternut squash, peeled
- 1 tsp cinnamon
- 1 tbsp olive oil

Directions:

1. Switch on the air fryer, insert the fryer basket, grease it with olive oil, then shut its lid, set the fryer at 220°F and preheat for 5 minutes.
2. Meanwhile, peel squash, cut it into 1-inch pieces, and then place them in a bowl.
3. Drizzle oil over squash pieces, sprinkle with cinnamon and then toss until well coated.
4. Open the fryer, add squash pieces to it, close with its lid and cook for 17 minutes until nicely golden and crispy, shaking every 5 minutes.
5. When the air fryer beeps, open its lid, transfer squash onto a serving plate and serve.

Nutrition:

- **Calories:** 179
- **Carbohydrates:** 22 g
- **Fat:** 3 g
- **Protein:** 1 g

39. Roasted Chickpeas

Preparation Time: 35 minutes

Cooking Time: 25 minutes

Servings: 6

Ingredients:

- 15-oz cooked chickpeas
- 1 tsp garlic powder
- 1 tbsp nutritional yeast
- $1/8$ tsp cumin
- 1 tsp smoked paprika
- ½ tsp salt
- 1 tbsp olive oil

Directions:

1. Take a large baking sheet, line it with paper towels, then spread chickpeas on it, cover peas with paper towels, and let rest for 30 minutes or until the chickpeas are dried.
2. Then switch on the air fryer, insert the fryer basket, grease it with olive oil, then shut its lid, set the fryer at 355°F, and preheat for 5 minutes.
3. Place dried chickpeas in a bowl, add remaining ingredients and toss until well coated.
4. Add chickpeas to the fryer, close with its lid, and cook for 20 minutes until nicely golden and crispy, shaking chickpeas every 5 minutes.
5. When the air fryer beeps, open its lid, transfer chickpeas onto a serving bowl, and serve.

Nutrition:

- **Calories:** 124
- **Carbohydrates:** 17.4 g
- **Fat:** 4.4 g
- **Protein:** 4.7 g

40. Cabbage Wedges

Preparation Time: 10 minutes

Cooking Time: 29 minutes

Servings: 6

Ingredients:

- 1 small head of green cabbage
- 6 strips of bacon, thick-cut, pastured
- 1 tsp onion powder
- ½ tsp pepper
- 1 tsp garlic powder
- ¾ tsp salt
- ¼ tsp red chili flakes
- ½ tsp fennel seeds
- 3 tbsp olive oil

Directions:

1. Switch on the air fryer, insert the fryer basket, grease it with olive oil, then shut its lid, set the fryer at 350°F and preheat for 5 minutes.
2. Add bacon strips to the fryer, close with its lid, and cook for 10 minutes until nicely golden and crispy, turning the bacon halfway through frying.
3. Meanwhile, prepare cabbage and for this, remove the outer leaves of the cabbage and then cut it into eight wedges, keeping the core intact.
4. Prepare spice mix and for this, place onion powder in a bowl, add black pepper, garlic powder, salt, red chili, and fennel and stir until mixed.
5. Drizzle cabbage wedges with oil and then sprinkle with spice mix until well coated.
6. When the air fryer beeps, open its lid, transfer bacon strips to a cutting board and let it rest.
7. Add seasoned cabbage wedges into the fryer basket, close with its lid, and then cook for 8 minutes at 400°F, flip cabbage, spray with oil and continue air frying for 6 minutes until nicely golden and cooked.
8. When done, transfer cabbage wedges to a plate.
9. Chop bacon, sprinkle it over cabbage and serve.

Nutrition:

- **Calories:** 123
- **Carbohydrates:** 2 g
- **Fat:** 11 g
- **Protein:** 4 g

41.   Buffalo Cauliflower Wings

Preparation Time: 5 minutes

Cooking Time: 30 minutes

Servings: 6

Ingredients:

- 1 tbsp almond flour
- 1 medium head of cauliflower
- 1 ½ tsp salt
- 4 tbsp hot sauce
- 1 tbsp olive oil

Directions:

1. Switch on the air fryer, insert the fryer basket, grease it with olive oil, then shut its lid, set the fryer at 400°F and preheat for 5 minutes.
2. Meanwhile, cut cauliflower into bite-size florets and set it aside.
3. Place flour in a large bowl, whisk in salt, oil, and hot sauce until combined, add cauliflower florets and toss until combined.
4. Open the fryer, add cauliflower florets in a single layer, close with its lid and cook for 15 minutes until nicely golden and crispy, shaking halfway through frying.
5. When the air fryer beeps, open its lid, transfer cauliflower florets onto a serving plate and keep warm.
6. Cook the remaining cauliflower florets in the same manner and serve.

Nutrition:

- **Calories:** 48
- **Carbohydrates:** 1 g
- **Fat:** 4 g
- **Protein:** 1 g

42.   Sweet Potato Cauliflower Patties

Preparation Time: 20 minutes

Cooking Time: 40 minutes

Servings: 7

Ingredients:

- 1 green onion, chopped
- 1 large sweet potato, peeled
- 1 tsp minced garlic
- 1 cup cilantro leaves
- 2 cups cauliflower florets
- ¼ tsp pepper
- ¼ tsp salt

- ¼ cup sunflower seeds
- ¼ tsp cumin
- ¼ cup ground flaxseed
- ½ tsp red chili powder
- 2 tbsp ranch seasoning mix
- 2 tbsp arrowroot starch

Directions:

1. Cut peeled sweet potato into small pieces, then place them in a food processor and pulse until pieces are broken up.
2. Then add onion, cauliflower florets, and garlic, pulse until combined, add remaining ingredients and pulse more until incorporated.
3. Tip mixture in a bowl, shape mixture into seven 1 ½ inch thick patties, each about ¼ cup, then place them on a baking sheet and freeze for 10 minutes.
4. Switch on the air fryer, insert the fryer basket, grease it with olive oil, then shut its lid, set the fryer at 400°F and preheat for 10 minutes.
5. Open the fryer, add patties in it in a single layer, close with its lid and cook for 20 minutes until nicely golden and cooked, flipping the patties halfway through frying.
6. When the air fryer beeps, open its lid, transfer patties onto a serving plate, and keep them warm.
7. Cook the remaining patties in the same manner and serve.

Nutrition:

- **Calories:** 85
- **Carbohydrates:** 9 g
- **Fat:** 3 g
- **Protein:** 2.7 g

43.   Okra

Preparation Time: 10 minutes

Cooking Time: 10 minutes

Servings: 4

Ingredients:

- 1 cup almond flour

- 8 oz fresh okra
- ½ tsp salt
- 1 cup milk, reduced-fat
- 1 egg, pastured

Directions:

1. Crack the egg in a bowl, pour in the milk, and whisk until blended.
2. Cut the stem from each okra, then cut it into ½-inch pieces, add them to the egg, and stir until well coated.
3. Mix flour and salt and add them into a large plastic bag.
4. Working on one okra piece at a time, drain each okra well by letting excess egg drip off, add it to the flour mixture, then seal the bag and shake well until each okra is well coated.
5. Place coated okra on a grease air fryer basket, coat the remaining okra pieces in the same manner and place them into the basket.
6. Switch on the air fryer, insert the fryer basket, spray okra with oil, then shut its lid, set the fryer at 390°F, and cook for 10 minutes until nicely golden and cooked, stirring okra halfway through frying.
7. Serve straight away.

Nutrition:

- **Calories:** 250
- **Carbohydrates:** 38 g
- **Fat:** 9 g
- **Protein:** 3 g

44.   Creamed Spinach

Preparation Time: 10 minutes

Cooking Time: 20 minutes

Servings: 2

Ingredients:

- ½ cup chopped white onion
- 10 oz frozen spinach, thawed
- 1 tsp salt
- 1 tsp pepper
- 2 tsp minced garlic

- ½ tsp ground nutmeg
- 4 oz cream cheese, reduced-fat, diced
- ¼ cup shredded parmesan cheese, reduced-fat
- Oil

Directions:

1. Switch on the air fryer, insert the fryer basket, grease it with olive oil, then shut its lid, set the fryer at 350°F and preheat for 5 minutes.
2. Meanwhile, take a 6-inches baking pan, grease it with oil and set aside.
3. Place spinach in a bowl, add remaining ingredients except for parmesan cheese, stir until well mixed, and then add the mixture into the prepared baking pan.
4. Open the fryer, add pan to it, close with its lid, and cook for 10 minutes until cooked and cheese has melted, stirring halfway through.
5. Then sprinkle parmesan cheese on top of spinach and continue air fryer for 5 minutes at 400°F until top is nicely golden and cheese has melted.
6. Serve straight away.

Nutrition:

- **Calories:** 273
- **Carbohydrates:** 8 g
- **Fat:** 23 g
- **Protein:** 8 g

45. Cheesy Eggplant

Preparation Time: 20 minutes

Cooking Time: 15 minutes

Servings: 4

Ingredients:

- ½ cup and 3 tbsp almond flour, divided
- 1.25-lb eggplant, ½-inch sliced
- 1 tbsp chopped parsley
- 1 tsp Italian seasoning
- 2 tsp salt
- 1 cup marinara sauce
- 1 egg, pastured

- 1 tbsp water
- 3 tbsp grated parmesan cheese, reduced-fat
- ¼ cup grated mozzarella cheese, reduced-fat

Directions:

1. Slice eggplant into ½-inch pieces, place them in a colander, sprinkle with 1 ½ tsp salt on both sides, and let it rest for 15 minutes.
2. Meanwhile, place ½ cup flour in a bowl, add egg and water and whisk until blended.
3. Place the remaining flour in a shallow dish, add salt, Italian seasoning, and parmesan cheese, and stir until mixed.
4. Switch on the air fryer, insert the fryer basket, grease it with olive oil, then shut its lid, set the fryer at 360°F, and preheat for 5 minutes.
5. Meanwhile, drain eggplant pieces, pat them dry, and then dip each slice into the egg mixture and coat with flour mixture.
6. Open the fryer, add coated eggplant slices in a single layer, close with its lid and cook for 8 minutes until nicely golden and cooked, flipping eggplant slices halfway through frying.
7. Then top each eggplant slice with a tbsp marinara sauce and some mozzarella cheese and continue air frying for 1 to 2 minutes or until the cheese has melted.
8. When the air fryer beeps, open its lid, transfer eggplants onto a serving plate, and keep them warm.
9. Cook the remaining eggplant slices in the same manner and serve.

Nutrition:

- **Calories:** 193
- **Carbohydrates:** 27 g
- **Fat:** 5.5 g
- **Protein:** 10 g

46. Cauliflower Rice

Preparation Time: 10 minutes

Cooking Time: 27 minutes

Servings: 3

Ingredients:

For tofu:

- 1 cup diced carrot
- 6 oz tofu, extra-firm, drained
- ½ cup diced white onion
- 2 tbsp soy sauce
- 1 tsp turmeric

For cauliflower:

- ½ cup chopped broccoli
- 3 cups cauliflower rice
- 1 tbsp minced garlic
- ½ cup frozen peas
- 1 tbsp minced ginger
- 2 tbsp soy sauce
- 1 tbsp apple cider vinegar
- 1 ½ tsp toasted sesame oil

Directions:

1. Switch on the air fryer, insert the fryer pan, grease it with olive oil, then shut its lid, set the fryer at 370°F, and preheat for 5 minutes.
2. Meanwhile, place tofu in a bowl, crumble it, then add the remaining ingredients and stir until mixed.
3. Open the fryer, add the tofu mixture to it, and spray with oil; close with its lid and cook for 10 minutes until nicely golden and crispy, stirring halfway through frying.
4. Meanwhile, place all ingredients for cauliflower in a bowl and toss until mixed.
5. When the air fryer beeps, open its lid, add the cauliflower mixture, shake the pan gently to mix, and continue cooking for 12 minutes, shaking halfway through frying.
6. Serve straight away.

Nutrition:

- **Calories:** 258.1
- **Carbohydrates:** 20.8 g
- **Fat:** 13 g
- **Protein:** 18.2 g

47. Brussels Sprouts

Preparation Time: 5 minutes

Cooking Time: 10 minutes

Servings: 2

Ingredients:

- 2 cups Brussels sprouts
- ¼ tsp salt
- 1 tbsp olive oil
- 1 tbsp apple cider vinegar

Directions:

1. Switch on the air fryer, insert the fryer basket, grease it with olive oil, then shut its lid, set the fryer at 400°F, and preheat for 5 minutes.
2. Meanwhile, cut sprouts lengthwise into ¼-inch thick pieces, add them to a bowl, add remaining ingredients and toss until well coated.
3. Open the fryer, add sprouts to it, close with its lid and cook for 10 minutes until crispy and cooked, shaking halfway through frying.
4. When the air fryer beeps, open its lid, transfer sprouts onto a serving plate, and serve.

Nutrition:

- **Calories:** 88
- **Carbohydrates:** 11 g
- **Fat:** 4.4 g
- **Protein:** 3.9 g

48. Green Beans

Preparation Time: 5 minutes

Cooking Time: 13 minutes

Servings: 4

Ingredients:

- 1-lb green beans
- ¾ tsp garlic powder
- ¾ tsp pepper
- 1 ¼ tsp salt
- ½ tsp paprika

- Olive oil

Directions:

1. Switch on the air fryer, insert the fryer basket, grease it with olive oil, then shut its lid, set the fryer at 400°F, and preheat for 5 minutes.
2. Meanwhile, place beans in a bowl, spray generously with olive oil, sprinkle with garlic powder, black pepper, salt, and paprika and toss until well coated.
3. Open the fryer, add green beans to it, close with its lid and cook for 8 minutes until nicely golden and crispy, shaking halfway through frying.
4. When the air fryer beeps, open its lid, transfer green beans onto a serving plate and serve.

Nutrition:

- **Calories:** 45
- **Carbohydrates:** 7 g
- **Fat:** 1 g
- **Protein:** 2 g

49.   Asparagus Soup

Preparation Time: 10 minutes

Cooking Time: 20 minutes

Servings: 4

Ingredients:

- 1 avocado, peeled, pitted, cubed
- 12 oz asparagus
- ½ tsp pepper
- 1 tsp garlic powder
- 1 tsp salt
- 2 tbsp olive oil, divided
- ½ lemon, juiced
- 2 cups vegetable stock

Directions:

1. Switch on the air fryer, insert the fryer basket, grease it with olive oil, then shut its lid, set the fryer at 425°F, and preheat for 5 minutes.

2. Meanwhile, place asparagus in a shallow dish, drizzle with 1 tbsp oil, sprinkle with garlic powder, salt, and black pepper, and toss until well mixed.
3. Open the fryer, add asparagus to it, close with its lid and cook for 10 minutes until nicely golden and roasted, shaking halfway through frying.
4. When the air fryer beeps, open its lid and transfer the asparagus to a food processor.
5. Add remaining ingredients into a food processor and pulse until well combined and smooth.
6. Tip soup in a saucepan, pour in water if the soup is too thick, and heat it over medium-low heat for 5 minutes until thoroughly heated.
7. Ladle soup into bowls and serve.

Nutrition:

- **Calories:** 208
- **Carbohydrates:** 13 g
- **Fat:** 16 g
- **Protein:** 6 g

50.   Crunchy Brussels Sprouts

Preparation Time: 9 minutes

Cooking Time: 18 minutes

Servings: 2

Ingredients:

- 1 tsp avocado oil
- ½ tsp each black pepper (ground) and salt
- 10 oz brussels sprouts (halved)
- ⅓ tsp balsamic vinegar

Directions:

1. Heat the air fryer at 175°C.
2. Mix salt, vinegar, pepper, and oil together in a bowl. Add sprouts and toss.
3. Fry Brussels sprouts in the air fryer for 5 minutes.

Nutrition:

- **Calories:** 92

- **Protein:** 5.2 g
- **Carbohydrates:** 12.1 g
- **Fat:** 3.1 g

51.   Buffalo Cauliflower

Preparation Time: 11 minutes

Cooking Time: 14 minutes

Servings: 4

Ingredients:

- 1 large cauliflower
- 1 cup flour
- ¼ tsp each chili powder, cayenne, and pepper paprika
- 1 cup soy milk
- 2 tbsp butter
- 2 garlic cloves (minced)
- ½ cup cayenne pepper sauce
- 1 serving of cooking spray

Directions:

1. Cut cauliflower into small pieces. Rinse under cold water and drain.
2. Mix the flour, chili powder, cayenne, and paprika in a bowl. Add milk slowly for making a thick batter.
3. Add pieces of cauliflower to the batter and coat well.
4. Cook cauliflower in the air fryer for 20 minutes. Toss cauliflower and cook again for 10 minutes.
5. Take a saucepan and heat butter in it. Add garlic and hot sauce. Boil the sauce mixture and simmer for 2 minutes.
6. Transfer the cauliflower to a large bowl and pour the prepared sauce over the cooked cauliflower. Toss for combining.
7. Serve hot.

Nutrition:

- **Calories:** 190
- **Protein:** 12.3 g
- **Carbohydrates:** 2.3 g
- **Fat:** 12 g

52.   Stuffed Mushrooms

Preparation Time: 12 minutes

Cooking Time: 18 minutes

Servings: 6

Ingredients:

- 15 button mushrooms
- 1 tsp olive oil
- ⅛ tsp salt
- ½ tsp black pepper (crushed)
- ⅓ tsp balsamic vinegar

For filling:

- ¼ cup each bell pepper and onion
- 2 tbsp cilantro, chopped
- 1 tbsp jalapeno, chopped finely
- ½ cup mozzarella cheese, grated
- 1 tsp coriander, ground
- ¼ tsp each paprika and salt

Directions:

1. Use a damp cloth for cleaning mushrooms. Remove stems for making caps hollow.
2. Take a bowl and season mushroom caps with salt, oil, balsamic vinegar, and black pepper.
3. Take another bowl and mix ingredients for filling.
4. Use a spoon for filling mushroom caps. Press filling in the mushroom using the back side of the spoon.
5. Cook mushrooms in the air fryer for 10 minutes.
6. Serve hot.

Nutrition:

- **Calories:** 42
- **Protein:** 3.1 g
- **Carbohydrates:** 2.9 g
- **Fat:** 1.2 g

53.   Cauliflower Curry

Preparation Time: 8 minutes

Cooking Time: 13 minutes

Servings: 3

Ingredients:

- 1 cup vegetable stock
- ¾ cup coconut milk (light)
- 2 tsp curry powder
- 1 tsp garlic puree
- ½ tsp turmeric
- 12 oz cauliflower, cut in florets
- 1 ½ cup sweet corn kernels
- 3 spring onions, sliced
- Salt

For topping:

- Lime wedges
- 2 tbsp dried cranberries

Directions:

1. Heat your air fryer at 190°C.
2. Mix all ingredients in a large bowl. Combine well.
3. Transfer the cauliflower mixture to the air fryer basket.
4. Cook for 15 minutes. Give it a mix in middle.

Nutrition:

- **Calories:** 160
- **Protein:** 5.2 g
- **Carbohydrates:** 27.2 g
- **Fat:** 3.1 g

54. Air-Fried Avocado Wedges

Preparation Time: 3 minutes

Cooking Time: 18 minutes

Servings: 2

Ingredients:

- ¼ cup flour
- ½ tsp black pepper, ground
- ¼ tsp salt
- 1 tsp water
- 1 ripe avocado (cut into eight slices)

- ½ cup breadcrumbs
- 1 serving of cooking spray

Directions:

1. Heat your air fryer at 200°C.
2. Combine pepper, salt, and flour in a bowl. Place water in another bowl.
3. Take a shallow dish and spread breadcrumbs.
4. Coat avocado slices in flour mixture and dip them in water.
5. Coat slices in bread crumbs. Make sure both sides are evenly coated.
6. Use the cooking spray for misting slices of avocado.
7. Cook coated slices of avocado for four minutes. Flip slices and cook again for 3 minutes.
8. Serve hot.

Nutrition:

- **Calories:** 302
- **Protein:** 8.3 g
- **Carbohydrates:** 37.2 g
- **Fat:** 17.3 g

55. Buffalo Chickpeas

Preparation Time: 14 minutes

Cooking Time: 21 minutes

Servings: 2

Ingredients:

- 1 can chickpeas, rinsed
- 2 tbsp buffalo wing sauce
- 1 tbsp ranch dressing mix, dry

Directions:

1. Heat your air fryer at 175°C.
2. Use paper towels for removing excess moisture from chickpeas.
3. Transfer chickpeas to a bowl and add wing sauce. Add dressing mix and combine well.
4. Cook chickpeas in the air fryer for 8 minutes. Shake the basket and cook for 5 minutes.
5. Let chickpeas sit for 2 minutes.

6. Serve warm.

Nutrition:

- **Calories:** 172
- **Protein:** 7.2 g
- **Carbohydrates:** 31.6 g
- **Fat:** 1.4 g

56. Green Beans and Spicy Sauce

Preparation Time: 7 minutes

Cooking Time: 29 minutes

Servings: 4

Ingredients:

- 1 cup beer
- 1 ½ cup flour
- 2 tsp salt
- ½ tsp black pepper, ground
- 12 oz green beans, trimmed

For sauce:

- 1 cup ranch dressing
- 2 tsp sriracha sauce
- 1 tsp horseradish

Directions:

1. Mix the flour, beer, pepper, and salt in a mixing bowl. Add beans to the batter and coat well. Shake off extra batter.
2. Line the air fryer basket with parchment paper. Add beans and cook for 10 minutes. Shake in between.
3. Combine sriracha sauce, ranch dressing, and horscradish together in a bowl.
4. Serve beans with sauce by side.

Nutrition:

- **Calories:** 460.2
- **Protein:** 5.7 g
- **Carbohydrates:** 34.4 g
- **Fat:** 30.6 g

57. Cheesy Sugar Snap Peas

Preparation Time: 5 minutes

Cooking Time: 13 minutes

Servings: 4

Ingredients:

- ½ lb sugar snap peas
- 1 tsp olive oil
- ¼ cup breadcrumbs
- ½ cup parmesan cheese
- Pepper and salt, for seasoning
- 2 tbsp garlic, minced

Directions:

1. Remove the stem from each pea pod. Rinse peas and drain water.
2. Toss peas with breadcrumbs, olive oil, pepper, salt, and half of the cheese.
3. Cook peas in the air fryer for 4 minutes at 175°C.
4. Add minced garlic and cook again for 5 minutes.
5. Serve peas with the remaining cheese on top.

Nutrition:

- **Calories:** 72
- **Protein:** 5.7 g
- **Carbohydrates:** 8.9 g
- **Fat:** 3.3 g

58. Kiwi Chips

Preparation Time: 5 minutes

Cooking Time: 61 minutes

Servings: 6

Ingredients:

- 1 kg kiwi
- ½ tsp cinnamon, ground
- ¼ tsp nutmeg, ground

Directions:

1. Slice kiwi thinly. Keep them in a bowl.

2. Sprinkle nutmeg and cinnamon on top. Toss for mixing.
3. Preheat the air fryer to 165°C.
4. Cook kiwi in the air fryer for half an hour. Make sure you shake the basket halfway.
5. Let the chips cool down in the basket for 15 minutes.
6. Cool before serving.

Nutrition:

- **Calories:** 110
- **Protein:** 2.1 g
- **Carbohydrates:** 26.3 g
- **Fat:** 1.1 g

59.   Apple Crisp

Preparation Time: 9 minutes

Cooking Time: 18 minutes

Servings: 2

Ingredients:

- 2 apples, chopped
- 1 tsp each lemon juice and cinnamon
- 2 tbsp brown sugar

For topping:

- 3 tbsp flour
- 3 tbsp brown sugar
- ½ tsp salt
- 4 tbsp rolled oats
- 1 ½ tbsp butter

Directions:

1. Heat your air fryer at 170°C. Use butter for greasing the basket.
2. Combine lemon juice, apples, cinnamon, and sugar in a bowl.
3. Cook mixture for 15 minutes. Shake the basket and cook again for 5 minutes.
4. Mix sugar, flour, salt, butter, and oats for the topping. Use an electric mixer for mixing.
5. Scatter the topping over cooked apples.
6. Return the basket to the air fryer. Cook again for 5 minutes.

Nutrition:

- **Calories:** 341
- **Protein:** 3.9 g
- **Carbohydrates:** 60.5 g
- **Fat:** 12.3 g

60.   Roasted Veggies

Preparation Time: 6 minutes

Cooking Time: 24 minutes

Servings: 4

Ingredients:

- ½ cup of each summer squash, zucchini, mushrooms, cauliflower, asparagus, and sweet red pepper, diced
- 2 tsp vegetable oil
- ¼ tsp salt
- ½ tsp black pepper, ground
- 1 tsp seasoning

Directions:

1. Preheat the air fryer to 180°C.
2. Mix all veggies, oil, pepper, seasoning, and salt in a bowl. Toss well for coating.
3. Cook the mixture of veggies in the air fryer for 10 minutes.

Nutrition:

- **Calories:** 35
- **Protein:** 1.3 g
- **Carbohydrates:** 3.3 g
- **Fat:** 2.6 g

61.   Tempura Vegetables

Preparation Time: 9 minutes

Cooking Time: 34 minutes

Servings: 4

Ingredients:

- ½ cup of each flour, green beans, onion rings, asparagus spears, sweet pepper rings, zucchini slices, and avocado wedges
- ½ tsp each black pepper (ground) and salt
- 2 large eggs
- 2 tbsp water
- 1 cup panko breadcrumbs

- 2 tsp vegetable oil

Directions:

1. Combine flour, pepper, and ¼ tsp salt in a dish.
2. Combine water and eggs in a shallow dish.
3. Mix oil and breadcrumbs in another shallow dish.
4. Sprinkle remaining salt over veggies.
5. Dip veggies in the mixture of flour, then in the mixture of egg, and then coat in breadcrumbs.
6. Cook veggies in the air fryer for ten minutes. Shake in between.

Nutrition:

- **Calories:** 242
- **Protein:** 9.2 g
- **Carbohydrates:** 35.6 g
- **Fat:** 9.3 g

Chapter 5. Grains and Beans

62. Air Fried Veggie Quesadillas

Preparation Time: 21 minutes

Cooking Time: 18 minutes

Servings: 4

Ingredients:

- Cooking spray
- 4 whole-grain flour tortillas
- 4 oz reduced-fat sharp cheddar cheese,
- 2 tbsp chopped fresh cilantro
- 2 oz plain reduced-fat Greek yogurt
- ¼ tsp ground cumin
- ½ cup drained refrigerated Pico de gallo
- 1 tsp lime zest plus 1 tbsp fresh juice (from 1 lime)
- 1 cup sliced zucchini
- 1 cup sliced red bell pepper
- 1 cup no-salt-added canned black beans, drained and rinsed

Directions:

1. Sprinkle 2 tbsp shredded cheese over half of each tortilla. After that, you can add cheese to the tortilla. Also, add black beans, slices of zucchini, and ¼ cup of red pepper slices to the tortilla as well.

2. Sprinkle the remaining cheese on the tortilla. Now, you can fold the tortilla into the shape of a half-moon. They will now become quesadillas. We hope you understand that quesadillas are tortillas with fillings.

3. Coat quesadillas with cooking spray and secure them with toothpicks.

4. Coat the air fryer basket with cooking spray. Then, you can place quesadillas in the basket. Cook them at 400°F until they turn golden brown and crispy. This should happen after about 10 minutes of cooking. Remember to turn the quesadillas over after 5 minutes. You can air fry all quesadillas at once or in two batches.

5. While quesadillas are being cooked, mix cumin, lime juice, lime zest, and yogurt in a bowl.

6. You need to cut each of the quesadillas into wedges before you serve them. It is also necessary to sprinkle cilantro on them. Serve each of them with 1 tbsp cumin and 2 tbsp Pico de Gallo

Nutrition:

- **Calories:** 291
- **Carbohydrates:** 12 g
- **Fat:** 8 g
- **Protein:** 17 g

63. Scrambled Tofu

Preparation Time: 7 minutes

Cooking Time: 18 minutes

Servings: 2

Ingredients:

- 4-6 whole wheat tortillas, warmed
- 2 14-oz blocks of extra-firm tofu
- 1 15-oz can of black beans, rinsed, drained
- 2 tbsp vegetable oil
- 1 onion, chopped

- ½ tsp ground cumin
- ½ tsp ground coriander
- 1 green bell pepper, chopped finely
- 1 red bell pepper, chopped finely
- 1 ½ tsp ground turmeric
- ¼ cup coarsely chopped fresh cilantro
- Salt
- Ground pepper

Garnishes:

- Salsa
- Scallions, sliced
- Cheddar, grated
- Avocado, chopped

Directions:

1. Smash tofu using a fork or potato masher.
2. Put onion and peppers in the Air fryer basket. Cook for 2 minutes. Season with cumin and coriander. Cook for 1 minute.
3. Add in tofu. Stir in turmeric. Add beans; cook for 1 to 2 minutes. Stir in cilantro; season with salt and pepper.
4. Serve with tortillas and garnishes.

Nutrition:

- **Calories:** 100
- **Carbohydrates:** 6 g
- **Fat:** 5 g
- **Protein:** 8 g

64. Easy Falafel

Preparation Time: 6 minutes

Cooking Time: 34 minutes

Servings: 15

Ingredients:

- 1 cup garbanzo beans
- 2 cups cilantro (remove stems)
- ¾ cup parsley (remove stems)
- 1 red onion, quartered
- 1 garlic clove
- 2 tbsp chickpea flour
- 1 tbsp of each cumin (ground), coriander (ground), and sriracha sauce

- 1 tsp black pepper and salt (for seasoning)
- ½ tsp each baking soda and baking powder
- 1 serving of cooking spray

Directions:

1. Soak beans in cool water for one day. Rub beans and remove the skin. Rinse in cold water and use paper towels for removing excess moisture.
2. Add cilantro, beans, onion, parsley, and garlic to a blender. Blend ingredients until paste forms.
3. Transfer the blended paste to a bowl and add coriander, flour, sriracha, cumin, pepper, and salt. Mix well. Let the mixture sit for 20 minutes.
4. Add baking soda and baking powder to the mixture. Mix well.
5. Make 15 balls from the mixture and flatten them using your hands for making patties.
6. Use a cooking spray for greasing falafel patties.
7. Cook them for 10 minutes.
8. Serve warm.

Nutrition:

- **Calories:** 57.9
- **Carbohydrates:** 8.9 g
- **Protein:** 3.2 g
- **Fat:** 1.4 g

65. Mini Cheese and Bean Tacos

Preparation Time: 9 minutes

Cooking Time: 23 minutes

Servings: 12

Ingredients:

- 1 can of refried beans
- 1 oz taco seasoning mix
- 12 slices of American cheese (halved)
- 12 tortillas
- 1 serving of cooking spray

Directions:

1. Place beans in a medium-sized bowl. Add seasoning mix. Combine well.
2. Place one cheese piece in the center of each tortilla. Take 1 tbsp bean mix and add it over the cheese. Add another cheese piece over the beans. Fold tortillas in half. Gently press with your hands for sealing the ends.
3. Use the cooking spray for spraying tacos.
4. Cook tacos for 3 minutes. Turn tacos and cook again for 3 minutes
5. Serve hot.

Nutrition:

- **Calories:** 229
- **Carbohydrates:** 20.2 g
- **Protein:** 11.3 g
- **Fat:** 10.4 g

66.   Crunchy Grains

Preparation Time: 9 minutes

Cooking Time: 16 minutes

Servings: 4

Ingredients:

- 3 cups whole grains, cooked
- ½ cup peanut oil

Directions:

1. Use a paper towel for removing excess moisture from grains.
2. Toss grains in oil.
3. Add coated grains to the basket of the air fryer. Cook for 10 minutes. Toss grains and cook again for 5 minutes.

Nutrition:

- **Calories:** 71
- **Carbohydrates:** 34.4 g
- **Protein:** 5.8 g
- **Fat:** 3.2 g

67.   Chicken and Mushrooms in Coconut Cream

Preparation Time: 5 minutes

Cooking Time: 28 minutes

Servings: 4

Ingredients:

- 1 can button mushrooms, rinsed well, large caps halved/quartered
- 1 ½ cup cooked Basmati rice
- $1/8$ cup fresh cilantro, minced

Chicken and marinade:

- 4 chicken thigh fillets, cubed
- ½ tbsp fresh ginger, peeled, grated
- 1 piece bird's eye chili, minced, optional
- 1 can thick coconut cream
- 1 tbsp fresh lemongrass bulb, tough parts peeled off, minced
- $1/16$ tsp salt
- $1/16$ tsp white pepper

Directions:

1. Preheat Air Fryer to 355°F. Cook the dish for 5 minutes.
2. Combine chicken and marinade in a large bowl. Set aside in the fridge for at least 30 minutes to steep. Divide into 2 equal portions.
3. To prepare the tiffin box, spread cooked rice evenly into the bottom of the tiffin box. Sprinkle mushrooms evenly on top.
4. Pour chicken and marinade on top of the mushrooms. Seal lid. Set aside until the chicken comes to room temperature.
5. Place sealed tiffin box into Air Fryer basket.
6. Turn down the heat to 285°F. Continue cooking for another 15 minutes. Turn off the machine immediately. Leave the tiffin box in the basket for 5 minutes to rest.
7. Remove the tiffin box. Carefully take off the lid. Garnish the dish with cilantro. Serve right out of the tiffin box

Nutrition:

- **Calories:** 174
- **Carbohydrates:** 8.4 g
- **Fat:** 4.5 g
- **Protein:** 24.1 g

68.   Honey Lemon Garlic Chicken

Preparation Time: 8 minutes

Cooking Time: 18 minutes

Servings: 4

Ingredients:

- 4 (5-oz / 142-g) low-sodium boneless, skinless chicken breasts, cut into 4-by-½-inch strips
- 2 tsp olive oil
- 2 tbsp cornstarch
- 3 garlic cloves, minced
- ½ cup low-sodium chicken broth
- ¼ cup freshly squeezed lemon juice
- 1 tbsp honey
- ½ tsp dried thyme
- Brown rice, cooked (optional)

Directions:

1. In a large bowl, mix chicken and olive oil. Sprinkle with cornstarch. Toss to coat.
2. Add garlic and transfer to a baking pan. Bake in the air fryer at 400°F (204°C) for 10 minutes, stirring once during cooking.
3. Add chicken broth, lemon juice, honey, and thyme to the chicken mixture. Bake for 6 to 9 minutes more, or until sauce is slightly thickened and chicken reaches an internal temperature of 165°F (74°C) on a meat thermometer. Serve over hot cooked brown rice, if desired.

Nutrition:

- **Calories:** 214
- **Carbohydrates:** 10 g
- **Fat:** 4 g
- **Protein:** 33 g

69.   South Indian Pepper Chicken

Preparation Time: 22 minutes

Cooking Time: 18 minutes

Servings: 4

Ingredients:

Spice mix:

- 1 dried red chili or ½ tsp dried red pepper flakes
- 1-inch piece of cinnamon or cassia bark
- 1 ½ tsp coriander seeds
- 1 tsp fennel seeds
- 1 tsp cumin seeds
- 1 tsp black peppercorns
- ½ tsp cardamom seeds
- ¼ tsp ground turmeric
- 1 tsp salt

Chicken:

- 1 lb (454 g) boneless, skinless chicken thighs
- 2 medium onions, cut into ½-inch-thick slices
- ¼ cup olive oil
- Cauliflower rice, steamed rice, or naan bread, for serving

Directions:

1. **For the spice mix:** Combine dried chili, cinnamon, coriander, fennel, cumin, peppercorns, and cardamom in a clean coffee or spice grinder. Grind, shaking the grinder lightly, so all seeds and bits get into blades until the mixture is broken down to a fine powder. Stir in turmeric and salt.
2. **For the chicken:** Place chicken and onions in a resealable plastic bag. Add oil and 1½ tbsp of the spice mix. Seal the bag and massage until the chicken is well coated. Marinate at room temperature for 30 minutes or in the refrigerator for up to 24 hours.
3. Place chicken and onions in the air fryer basket. Bake at 350°F (177°C) for 10 minutes, stirring once halfway through cooking time. Increase temperature to 400°F (204°C) and bake for 5 minutes more.

4. Serve with steamed rice, cauliflower rice, or naan.

Nutrition:

- **Calories:** 254
- **Carbohydrates:** 1 g
- **Fat:** 18 g
- **Protein:** 22 g

70. Creamy Chicken, Peas, and Rice

Preparation Time: 10 minutes

Cooking Time: 30 minutes

Servings: 4

Ingredients:

- 1 lb chicken breasts; skinless, boneless, and cut into quarters
- 1 cup white rice; already cooked
- 1 cup chicken stock
- ¼ cup parsley; chopped.
- 2 cups peas; frozen
- 1 ½ cups parmesan; grated
- 1 tbsp olive oil
- 3 garlic cloves; minced
- 1 yellow onion; chopped
- ½ cup white wine
- ¼ cup heavy cream
- Salt and black pepper to taste

Directions:

1. Season chicken with salt and pepper, drizzle half of the oil over them, rub well, put in your air fryer's basket, and cook them at 360°F for 6 minutes.
2. Preheat the pan with the rest of the oil over medium-high heat; add garlic, onion, wine, stock, salt, pepper, and heavy cream; stir and simmer. Cook for 9 minutes.
3. Transfer chicken breasts into a heat-proof dish that fits your air fryer, add peas, rice, and cream mix over them, toss, and sprinkle parmesan and parsley all over, place in your air fryer and cook at 420°F for

10 minutes. Divide among plates and serve hot.

Nutrition:

- **Calories:** 313
- **Carbohydrates:** 27 g
- **Fat:** 12 g
- **Protein:** 44 g

71. Best Ever Jalapeño Poppers

Preparation Time: 10 minutes

Cooking Time: 10 minutes

Servings: 4

Ingredients:

- 12 to 18 whole fresh jalapeño
- 1 cup nonfat refried beans
- 1 cup shredded Monterrey jack
- 1 scallion
- 1 tsp salt, divided
- ¼ cup all-purpose flour
- 2 large eggs
- ½ cup fine cornmeal
- Olive oil or canola oil cooking spray

Directions:

1. Start by slicing each jalapeño lengthwise on one side. Place jalapeños side by side in a microwave-safe bowl and microwave them until they are slightly soft, usually around 5 minutes.
2. While your jalapeños cook, mix the refried beans, scallions, ½ tsp salt, and cheese in a bowl.
3. Once your jalapeños are softened, you can scoop out the seeds and add 1 tbsp of your refried bean mixture (it can be a little less if the pepper is smaller.) Press jalapeño closed around the filling.
4. Beat eggs in a small bowl and place your flour in a separate bowl. In a third bowl, mix your cornmeal and remaining salt in a third bowl.

5. Roll each pepper in flour, then dip it in egg, and finally roll it in cornmeal, making sure to coat the entire pepper.

6. Place peppers on a flat surface and coat them with a cooking spray; olive oil cooking spray is suggested.

7. Pour into oven rack/basket. Place rack on middle-shelf of Cosori air fryer oven. Set temperature to 400°F and set time to 5 minutes. Select start/stop to begin. Turn each pepper, and then cook for another 5 minutes; serve hot.

Nutrition:

- **Calories:** 244
- **Fat:** 12 g
- **Carbohydrates:** 22 g
- **Protein:** 12 g
- **Fiber:** 2.4 g

72. Sweet Potato Lentil Stew

Preparation Time: 10 minutes

Cooking Time: 30 minutes

Servings: 6

Ingredients:

- ½ tsp ground cumin
- ¼ tsp ground ginger
- ¼ tsp cayenne pepper
- 1 ¼ lb sweet potatoes cut into pieces
- 1 ½ cups dried lentils, rinsed
- 3 medium carrots, cut into pieces
- 1 medium onion, chopped
- 4 garlic cloves, minced
- 1 carton of vegetable broth
- ¼ cup minced fresh cilantro

Directions:

1. Ready Air Fryer to 400°F.

2. Merge the first 9 ingredients.

3. Prepare in the fryer basket and cook for at least 30 minutes.

4. Top with cilantro.

5. Serve and enjoy!

Nutrition:

- **Calories:** 116
- **Carbohydrates:** 23 g
- **Fat:** 1 g
- **Protein:** 4 g

73. Quick Paella

Preparation Time: 7 minutes

Cooking Time: 13 to 17 minutes

Servings: 4

Ingredients:

- 1 (10-oz) package frozen cooked rice, thawed
- 1 (6-oz) jar of artichoke hearts
- ¼ cup vegetable broth
- ½ tsp turmeric
- ½ tsp dried thyme
- 1 cup frozen cooked small shrimp
- ½ cup frozen baby peas
- 1 tomato, diced

Directions:

1. In a 6-by-6-by-2-inch pan, combine rice, artichoke hearts, vegetable broth, turmeric, and thyme, and stir gently.

2. Prepare and put in the air fryer. Cook for 9 minutes or until the rice is hot.

3. Remove from the air fryer and gently stir in shrimp, peas, and tomato. Cook for 5 to 8 minutes or until the shrimp and peas are hot and the paella is bubbling.

Nutrition:

- **Calories:** 345
- **Carbohydrates:** 66 g

- **Fat:** 1 g
- **Protein:** 18 g

74. Sea Bass Paella

Preparation Time: 10 minutes

Cooking Time: 25 minutes

Servings: 4

Ingredients:

- 1 lb sea bass fillets; cubed
- 1 red bell pepper; deseeded and chopped.
- 6 scallops
- 8 shrimps, peeled and deveined
- 5 oz wild rice
- 2 oz peas
- 14 oz dry white wine
- 3 ½ oz chicken stock
- A drizzle of olive oil
- Salt and black pepper, to taste

Directions:

1. In a heatproof dish that fits your air fryer, place all ingredients and toss.
2. Place the dish in your air fryer and cook at 380°F for 25 minutes, stirring halfway.
3. Divide between plates and serve.

Nutrition:

- **Calories:** 710
- **Carbohydrates:** 68 g
- **Fat:** 37 g
- **Protein:** 51 g

75. Brown Rice, Spinach, and Tofu Frittata

Preparation Time: 5 minutes

Cooking Time: 55 minutes

Servings: 4

Ingredients:

- ½ cup baby spinach, chopped
- ½ cup kale, chopped
- ½ onion, chopped
- ½ tsp turmeric
- 1 ¾ cups brown rice, cooked
- 1 flax egg (1 tbsp flaxseed meal + 3 tbsp cold water)
- 1 package of firm tofu
- 1 tbsp olive oil
- 1 yellow pepper, chopped
- 2 tbsp soy sauce
- 2 tsp arrowroot powder
- 2 tsp Dijon mustard
- $^2/_3$ cup almond milk
- 3 big mushrooms, chopped
- 3 tbsp nutritional yeast
- 4 cloves garlic, crushed
- 4 spring onions, chopped
- A handful of basil leaves, chopped

Directions:

1. Preheat the Cosori air fryer oven to 375°F. Grease a plan that will fit inside the Cosori air fryer oven.
2. Prepare frittata crust by mixing brown rice and flax egg. Press rice onto the baking dish until you form a crust. Brush with a little oil and cook for 10 minutes.
3. Meanwhile, heat olive oil in a skillet over medium flame and sauté garlic and onions for 2 minutes.
4. Add pepper and mushroom and continue stirring for 3 minutes.
5. Stir in kale, spinach, spring onions, and basil. Remove from pan and set aside.
6. Pulse together tofu, mustard, turmeric, soy sauce, nutritional yeast, vegan milk, and arrowroot powder in a food processor. Pour in a mixing bowl and stir in sautéed vegetables.
7. Pour the vegan frittata mixture over the rice crust and cook in the Cosori air fryer oven for 40 minutes.

Nutrition:

- **Calories:** 226

- **Carbohydrates:** 24 g
- **Fat:** 8.05 g
- **Protein:** 10.6 g

76.   Beef and Broccoli

Preparation Time: 10 minutes

Cooking Time: 14 to 18 minutes

Servings: 4

Ingredients:

- 2 tbsp cornstarch
- ½ cup low-sodium beef broth
- 1 tsp low-sodium soy sauce
- 12 oz sirloin strip steak, cut into 1-inch cubes
- 2 ½ cups broccoli florets
- 1 onion, chopped
- 1 cup sliced cremini mushrooms
- 1 tbsp grated fresh ginger
- Brown rice, cooked (optional)

Directions:

1. In a medium bowl, stir together cornstarch, beef broth, and soy sauce.
2. Add beef and toss to coat. Let stand for 5 minutes at room temperature.
3. Transfer beef from the broth mixture into a medium metal bowl with a slotted spoon. Reserve broth.
4. Add broccoli, onion, mushrooms, and ginger to the beef. Place the bowl into the air fryer and cook for 12 to 15 minutes, or until beef reaches at least 145°F on a meat thermometer and vegetables are tender.
5. Add reserved broth and cook for 2 to 3 minutes more, or until sauce boils.
6. Serve immediately over hot cooked brown rice, if desired.

Nutrition:

- **Calories:** 240
- **Carbohydrates:** 11 g
- **Fat:** 6 g (23% of calories from fat)
- **Saturated Fat:** 2 g
- **Protein:** 19 g
- **Sodium:** 107 mg

- **Fiber:** 2 g

77.   Pineapple Pudding

Preparation Time: 10 minutes

Cooking Time: 5 minutes

Servings: 8

Ingredients:

- 1 tbsp avocado oil
- 1 cup rice
- 14 oz milk
- Sugar to taste
- 8 oz canned pineapple, chopped

Directions:

1. Mix oil, milk, and rice in your air fryer, stir, cover and cook on High for 3 minutes.
2. Add sugar and pineapple, stir, cover and cook on High for 2 minutes more.
3. Divide into dessert bowls and serve.

Nutrition:

- **Calories:** 154
- **Carbohydrates:** 14 g
- **Protein:** 8 g
- **Fat:** 4 g

78.   Easy Corn and Black Bean Salsa

Preparation Time: 10 minutes

Cooking Time: 10 minutes

Servings: 4

Ingredients:

- ½ (15-oz) can of corn, drained and rinsed
- ½ (15-oz) can of black beans, drained and rinsed
- ¼ cup chunky salsa
- 2 oz reduced-fat cream cheese, softened
- ¼ cup shredded reduced-fat cheddar cheese
- ½ tsp paprika
- ½ tsp ground cumin
- Salt and freshly pepper, to taste

Directions:

1. In a medium bowl, combine corn, black beans, cheddar cheese, cream cheese, salsa, cumin, and paprika. Sprinkle with salt and pepper and stir until well blended.
2. Pour the mixture into a baking dish.
3. Place baking dish in air fryer grill.
4. Select Air Fry, set the temperature to 325°F (163°C) and set time to 10 minutes.
5. When cooking is complete, the mixture should be heated through. Rest for 5 minutes and serve warm.

Nutrition:

- **Calories:** 108
- **Carbohydrates:** 17.4 g
- **Fat:** 1.4 g
- **Sugar:** 2.4 g
- **Protein:** 7.3 g
- **Cholesterol:** 0 mg

79. Beef Taco Roll-Ups with Cotija Cheese

Preparation Time: 5 minutes

Cooking Time: 25 minutes

Servings: 4

Ingredients:

- 1 tbsp sesame oil
- 2 tbsp scallions, chopped
- 1 garlic clove, minced
- 1 bell pepper, chopped
- ½ lb ground beef
- ½ tsp Mexican oregano
- ½ tsp dried marjoram
- 1 tsp chili powder
- ½ cup refried beans
- Salt and pepper, to taste
- ½ cup Cotija cheese, shredded
- 8 roll wrappers

Directions:

1. Start by preheating your Air Fryer to 395°F.

2. Heat sesame oil in a nonstick skillet over medium-high heat. Cook scallions, garlic, and peppers until tender and fragrant.
3. Add ground beef, oregano, marjoram, and chili powder. Continue cooking for 3 minutes longer or until it is browned.
4. Stir in beans, salt, and pepper. Divide the meat/bean mixture between wrappers that are softened with a little bit of water. Top with cheese.
5. Roll wrappers and spritz them with cooking oil on all sides.
6. Cook in preheated Air Fryer for 11 to 12 minutes, flipping them halfway through cooking Time. Enjoy!

Nutrition:

- **Calories:** 417
- **Carbohydrates:** 41 g
- **Fat:** 15.9 g
- **Protein:** 26.2 g
- **Sugars:** 1.5 g

80. Cheesy Sweet Potato and Bean Burritos

Preparation Time: 15 minutes

Cooking Time: 30 minutes

Servings: 6

Ingredients:

- 2 sweet potatoes
- 1 tbsp vegetable oil
- Salt and pepper, to taste
- 6 large flour tortillas
- 1 (16-oz / 454-g) can of refried black beans, divided
- 1 ½ cups baby spinach, divided
- 6 eggs, scrambled
- ¾ cup grated cheddar cheese, divided
- ¼ cup salsa
- ¼ cup sour cream
- Cooking spray

Directions:

1. Put sweet potatoes in a large bowl, then drizzle with vegetable oil and sprinkle with salt and black pepper. Toss to coat well.
2. Place potatoes in an air fry basket.
3. Place the basket on air fry position.
4. Select Air Fry, set the temperature to 400°F (205°C), and set the time to 10 minutes. Flip potatoes halfway through cooking time.
5. When done, potatoes should be lightly browned. Remove potatoes from the air fryer grill.
6. Unfold tortillas on a clean work surface. Divide air-fried sweet potatoes, black beans, spinach, scrambled eggs, and cheese on top of tortillas.
7. Fold the long side of the tortillas over the filling, then fold in the shorter side to wrap the filling to make burritos.
8. Wrap burritos in aluminum foil and put them in the basket.
9. Place the basket on air fry position.
10. Select Air Fry, set the temperature to 350°F (180°C) and set time to 20 minutes. Flip burritos halfway through cooking time.
11. Remove burritos from the air fryer grill and spread with sour cream and salsa. Serve immediately.

Nutrition:

- **Calories:** 133
- **Fat:** 19 g
- **Carbohydrates:** 20 g
- **Protein:** 8 g

81.   Black Bean Burger

Preparation Time: 10 minutes

Cooking Time: 25 minutes

Servings: 6

Ingredients:

- 1 ¼ cup rolled oats
- 16 oz black beans, rinsed and drained
- ¾ cup salsa
- 1 tbsp soy sauce

- 1 ¼ tsp chili powder
- ¼ tsp chipotle chili powder
- ½ tsp garlic powder

Directions:

1. Pulse oats inside a food processor until powdery.
2. Add all necessary ingredients and pulse until well blended.
3. Transfer to a bowl and refrigerate for 15 minutes.
4. Form into burger patties.
5. Cook in the air fryer at 375°F for 15 minutes.

Nutrition:

- **Calories:** 158
- **Total Carbohydrates:** 30 g
- **Total fat:** 2 g
- **Saturated fat:** 1 g
- **Cholesterol:** 10 mg
- **Sodium:** 690 mg
- **Dietary fiber:** 9 g
- **Total sugars:** 2.7 g
- **Protein:** 8 g
- **Potassium:** 351 mg

82.   Curry Chickpeas

Preparation Time: 15 minutes

Cooking Time: 35 minutes

Servings: 4

Ingredients:

- 1 (15-oz) can of no-salt-added chickpeas (garbanzo beans), drained and rinsed (about 1½ cups)
- 2 tbsp olive oil
- 2 tbsp red wine vinegar
- ¼ tsp ground coriander
- $1/_8$ tsp ground cinnamon
- ¼ tsp ground cumin
- 2 tsp curry powder
- ½ tsp ground turmeric
- Thinly sliced fresh cilantro
- ½ tsp Aleppo pepper
- ¼ tsp salt

Directions:

1. Smash chickpeas mildly in a medium bowl with your hands. Remove chick-pea skins.
2. Pour over oil and vinegar into chickpeas. Stir to coat evenly, and add coriander, cinnamon, cumin, curry powder, and turmeric. Stir the mixture gently to combine.
3. In the air fryer basket, arrange chick-peas in a single layer and allow cooking at 400°F for about 15 minutes or until the chickpeas are crispy. Ensure that you shake chickpeas after the first 7 or 8 minutes of cooking.
4. Move cooked chickpeas into a bowl while sprinkling cilantro, Aleppo pepper, and salt. Toss to coat.

Nutrition:

- **Calories:** 409
- **Fat:** 16.6 g
- **Carbohydrates:** 24 g
- **Protein:** 38.6 g
- **Sugar:** 17.2 g

83.   Ranchero Brunch Crunch Wraps

Preparation Time: 5 minutes

Cooking Time: 15 minutes

Servings: 2 crunch wraps

Ingredients:

- 2 servings tofu scramble (or vegan egg)
- 2 large flour tortillas
- 2 small corn tortillas
- ⅓ cup pinto beans, cooked
- ½ cup classic ranchero sauce
- ½ avocado, peeled and sliced
- 2 fresh jalapeños, stemmed and sliced

Directions:

1. Assemble large tortillas on a work surface. Arrange crunch wraps by stacking the following ingredients in order: tofu or egg scramble, jalapeños, ranchero sauce, corn tortillas, avocado, and pinto beans. You can add more ranchero sauce if desired.

2. Fold large flour tortilla around fillings until sealed completely.
3. Place one crunch wrap in the air fryer basket and set the basket on top of the trivet.
4. Air-fry each crunch wrap at 350°F (or 180°C) for 6 minutes. Remove from the basket and transfer to a plate.
5. Repeat steps 3 and 4 for another crunch wrap.

Nutrition:

- **Calories:** 290
- **Carbohydrates:** 26 g
- **Fat:** 14 g
- **Fiber:** 11 g
- **Protein:** 15 g
- **Sodium:** 340 mg
- **Sugar:** 3 g

84.   Best Air-Fried English Breakfast

Preparation Time: 5 minutes

Cooking Time: 20 minutes

Servings: 4

Ingredients:

- 8 sausages
- 8 bacon slices
- 4 eggs
- 1 (16-oz) can of baked beans
- 8 slices of toast

Directions:

1. Add sausages and bacon slices to your air fryer and cook them for 10 minutes at 320°F.
2. Using a ramekin or heat-safe bowl, add baked beans, then place another ramekin and add eggs, and whisk.
3. Increase temperature to 290°F.
4. Place inside your fryer and cook for additional 10 minutes or until everything is done.
5. Serve and enjoy!

Nutrition:

- **Calories:** 850
- **Carbohydrates:** 20 g
- **Fat:** 40 g
- **Protein:** 48 g

85.   Saltine Wax Beans

Preparation Time: 10 minutes

Cooking Time: 7 minutes

Servings: 4

Ingredients:

- ½ cup flour
- 1 tsp smoky chipotle powder
- ½ tsp pepper
- 1 tsp salt flakes
- 2 eggs, beaten
- ½ cup crushed saltines
- 10 oz (283 g) wax beans
- Cooking spray

Directions:

1. Preheat the air fryer oven to 360°F (182° C).

2. Combine flour, chipotle powder, black pepper, and salt in a bowl. Put eggs in the second bowl. Put crushed saltines in the third bowl.

3. Wash beans with cold water and discard any tough strings.

4. Coat beans with the flour mixture before dipping them into a beaten egg. Cover them with crushed saltines.

5. Spritz beans with cooking spray, then transfer to the air fryer basket.

6. Move the baking pan to the fryer basket and set the time to 4 minutes.

7. Give the air fryer basket a good shake and continue to air fry for 3 minutes. Serve hot.

Nutrition:

- **Calories:** 35
- **Carbohydrates:** 7 g
- **Fat:** 15.6 g
- **Fiber:** 3 g
- **Protein:** 2 g

86.   Manchester Stew

Preparation Time: 10 minutes

Cooking Time: 30 minutes

Servings: 6

Ingredients:

- 2 ½ cups water
- 1 can of no-salt-added diced tomatoes
- 1 tsp dried thyme
- ½ tsp salt and pepper
- 2 tbsp olive oil
- 2 medium onions, chopped
- 2 garlic cloves, minced
- 1 tsp dried oregano
- 1 cup dry red wine
- 1 lb small red potatoes, quartered
- 1 can kidney beans, rinsed and drained
- ½ lb sliced fresh mushrooms
- 2 medium leeks (white portion only), sliced
- 1 cup fresh baby carrots
- Basil, optional

Directions:

1. Preheat Air Fryer to 400°F. Merge garlic, onions, oil, oregano, and wine into Air Fryer.

2. Put potatoes, beans, mushrooms, leeks and carrots, water, tomatoes, thyme, salt, and pepper.

3. Cook for at least 30 minutes. Top with fresh basil.

4. Serve and enjoy!

Nutrition:

- **Calories:** 220
- **Carbohydrates:** 30 g
- **Fat:** 1 g
- **Protein:** 8 g

87.   Southwest Turkey Stew

Preparation Time: 15 minutes

Cooking Time: 30 minutes

Servings: 6

Ingredients:

- 1 ½ lb turkey breast tenderloins, cubed
- 2 tsp canola oil
- 1 can turkey chili with beans, undrained
- 1 can diced tomatoes, undrained
- 1 medium sweet red pepper, chopped
- 1 medium green pepper, chopped
- ¾ cup chopped onion
- ¾ cup salsa
- 3 garlic cloves, minced
- 1 ½ tsp chili powder
- ½ tsp ground cumin
- ¼ tsp salt

Directions:

1. Preheat the air fryer to 375°F. Mix turkey, chili, tomatoes, peppers, onion, salsa, garlic, chili powder, cumin, and salt in a small mixing bowl.

2. Place in the air fryer basket and cook for about 30 minutes.

3. Serve and enjoy!!!

Nutrition:

- **Calories:** 238
- **Carbohydrates:** 17 g
- **Fat:** 4 g
- **Protein:** 30 g

88.   Tomato Black Bean Soup

Preparation Time: 20 minutes

Cooking Time: 25 minutes

Servings: 6

Ingredients:

Soup:

- ½ medium white onion chopped
- 2 tbsp corn oil
- 4 cups of cooked black beans - puréed
- 3 Roma tomatoes, chopped
- 1 ancho chili, stemmed and seeded
- 1 ½ cups water
- 3 cloves garlic
- 2 ½ cups vegetable broth
- 1 tsp salt

Toppings:

- Tortilla chips or strips
- Chopped ripe Hass avocado
- Fried ancho chili strips
- Vegan sour cream

Directions:

1. Preheat Air Fryer to 400°F. Merge tomatoes, ancho, garlic, onion, and water in a small mixing bowl. Put in a blender and blend properly.

2. Sprinkle oil on the Air Fryer basket. Put the blended mixture and cook for about 5 minutes. Put pureed beans, vegetable broth, and salt.

3. Cook for another 10 minutes. Top with any topping of your choice.

4. Serve and enjoy!

Nutrition:

- **Calories:** 134

- **Carbohydrates:** 24 g
- **Fat:** 1 g
- **Protein:** 7 g

89. Beefy Cabbage Bean Stew

Preparation Time: 20 minutes

Cooking Time: 30 minutes

Servings: 6

Ingredients:

- 1 medium green pepper, chopped
- 1 small onion, chopped
- 3 garlic cloves, minced
- ½ lb lean ground beef
- 3 cups shredded cabbage
- 1 can red beans, rinsed and drained
- 1 can diced tomatoes, undrained
- 1 can (8 oz) tomato sauce
- ¾ cup salsa or picante sauce
- 1 tsp ground cumin
- ½ tsp pepper

Directions:

1. Preheat Air Fryer to 400°F.
2. Merge all ingredients into Air Fryer and cook for about 30 minutes.
3. Serve and enjoy!

Nutrition:

- **Calories:** 177
- **Carbohydrates:** 23 g
- **Fat:** 4 g
- **Protein:** 13 g

90. Spicy Chicken Stew

Preparation Time: 10 minutes

Cooking Time: 15 minutes

Servings: 6

Ingredients:

- 1 can of garbanzo beans rinsed and drained
- 1 can diced tomatoes with onions, undrained
- 1 cup lime-garlic salsa
- 2 lb boneless skinless chicken thighs, cut into pieces
- 2 tsp minced garlic
- 2 tbsp olive oil
- 1 tsp ground cumin
- ⅓ cup minced fresh cilantro

Directions:

1. Preheat Air Fryer to 400°F. Mix chicken, garlic, beans, and tomatoes with onions, cilantro, salsa, and cumin in a small mixing bowl.
2. Place them in the Air Fryer basket and cook for at least 15 minutes.
3. Serve and enjoy!

Nutrition:

- **Calories:** 250
- **Carbohydrates:** 30 g
- **Fat:** 6 g
- **Protein:** 17 g

91. Vegetable Soup

Preparation Time: 10 minutes

Cooking Time: 35 minutes

Servings: 4

Ingredients:

- 2 ml olive oil
- 1 stalk onion
- 3 tbsp chili powder
- 1 stalk carrot
- 2 stalk potatoes
- 300 g tomatoes

- 1 l vegetable soup
- 1 can of kidney beans
- 130 g peas
- 1 can corn
- 70 g fresh cream cheese
- 1 pinch salt
- 1 pinch pepper
- 1 shot salsa

Directions:

1. Heat oil in an air fryer and sauté chopped onions. Then add chili powder and mix well.

2. Then fry the chopped carrot, diced potatoes, and sliced tomatoes for 2 to 3 minutes. Add vegetables to soup and cook on medium with a lid for 20 minutes.

3. Finally add corn, peas, and beans and cook the soup for another 10 minutes.

4. To thicken the soup, add fresh cream and season with salt, pepper, and salsa.

Nutrition:

- **Calories:** 156
- **Carbohydrates:** 29 g
- **Fat:** 2 g
- **Protein:** 5 g

92. Sweet Potatoes with Baked Taquitos

Preparation Time: 5 minutes

Cooking Time: 41 minutes

Servings: 5

Ingredients:

- 1 sweet potato (cut in pieces of half an inch)
- 2 tsp canola oil
- ½ cup yellow onion (chopped)
- 1 garlic clove (minced)
- 2 cups black beans (rinsed)
- 1 chipotle pepper (chopped)

- ½ tsp each paprika, cumin, chili powder, and maple syrup
- $\frac{1}{8}$ tsp salt
- 3 tbsp water
- 10 corn tortillas

Directions:

1. Place pieces of sweet potatoes in an air fryer and toss them with some oil. Cook for 12 minutes. Make sure you shake the basket in between.
2. Take a skillet and heat some oil in it. Add garlic and onions. Sauté for 5 minutes until onions are translucent.
3. Add chipotle pepper, beans, paprika, cumin, chili powder, maple syrup, and salt. Add 2 tbsp water and mix all ingredients.
4. Add cooked potatoes and mix well.
5. Warm the corn tortillas in a skillet.
6. Put 2 tbsp beans and potato mixture in a row across corn tortillas. Grab one end of the corn tortillas and roll them. Tuck the end under the mixture of sweet potato and beans.
7. Place taquitos with seam side down in the basket. Spray taquitos with some oil. Air fry prepared taquitos for 10 minutes.
8. Serve hot.

Nutrition:

- **Calories:** 112
- **Carbohydrates:** 19.3 g
- **Protein:** 5.2 g
- **Fat:** 1.6 g

93. Daily Bean Dish

Preparation Time: 5 minutes

Cooking Time: 8 minutes

Servings: 4

Ingredients:

- 1 can (15 oz) pinto beans, drained
- ¼ cup tomato sauce
- 2 tbsp nutritional yeast
- 2 large garlic cloves, minced
- ½ tsp dried oregano

- ½ tsp cumin
- ¼ tsp salt
- ⅛ tsp pepper
- Cooking oil spray, as needed

Directions:

1. Preheat your air fryer to 392°F.
2. Take a medium bowl and add beans, tomato sauce, yeast, garlic, oregano, cumin, salt, and pepper and mix well
3. Take your baking pan and add oil; pour bean mixture
4. Transfer to the air fryer and bake for 4 minutes until cooked thoroughly with a slightly golden crust on top
5. Serve and enjoy!

Nutrition:

Calories: 284

Carbohydrates: 47 g

Fat: 4 g

Protein: 20 g

94. Fine 10-Minute Chimichanga

Preparation Time: 2 minutes

Cooking Time: 8 minutes

Servings: 4

Ingredients:

- 1 whole-grain tortilla
- ½ cup vegan refried beans
- ¼ cup grated vegan cheese
- Cooking oil spray as needed
- ½ cup fresh salsa
- 2 cups romaine lettuce, chopped
- Guacamole
- Chopped cilantro

Directions:

1. Preheat your air fryer to 392°F.
2. Lay tortilla on flat surface and place beans on center, top with cheese and wrap bottom up over filling, fold insides.
3. Roll all up and enclose beans inside.

4. Spray the air fryer cooking basket with oil and place the wrap inside the basket and fry for 5 minutes. Spray on top and cook for 2 to 3 minutes more.
5. Transfer to a plate and serve with salsa, lettuce, guacamole, and cilantro.
6. Enjoy!

Nutrition:

- **Calories:** 317
- **Carbohydrates:** 55 g
- **Fat:** 6 g
- **Protein:** 13 g

95. Great Taquito

Preparation Time: 5 minutes

Cooking Time: 7 minutes

Servings: 4

Ingredients:

- 8 corn tortillas
- Cooking oil spray as needed
- 1 (15 oz) can of vegan refried beans
- 1 cup shredded vegan cheese
- Guacamole
- Cashew cheese
- Vegan sour cream
- Fresh salsa

Directions:

1. Preheat your air fryer to 392°F.
2. Warm your tortilla and run them underwater for a second, transfer them to the air fryer cooking basket and cook for 1 minute
3. Remove to the flat surface and place equal amounts of beans at the center of each tortilla, top with vegan cheese
4. Roll tortilla sides up over filling, place seam side down in air fryer
5. Spray oil on top and cook for 7 minutes until golden brown
6. Serve and enjoy!

Nutrition:

- **Calories:** 420
- **Carbohydrates:** 80 g

- **Fat:** 5 g
- **Protein:** 2 g

Chapter 6. Fish & Seafood Recipes

96. Salmon Cakes in Air Fryer

Preparation Time: 9 minutes

Cooking Time: 11 minutes

Servings: 2

Ingredients:

- 8 oz fresh salmon fillet
- 1 egg
- $\frac{1}{8}$ tsp salt
- ¼ tsp garlic powder
- 1 sliced lemon

Directions:

1. In a bowl, chop salmon, add egg & spices.
2. Form tiny cakes.
3. Let the Air fryer preheat to 390°F. On the bottom of the air fryer bowl lay sliced lemons—place cakes on top.
4. Cook them for 7 minutes.

Nutrition:

- **Calories:** 194
- **Carbohydrates:** 1 g
- **Fat:** 9 g
- **Protein:** 25 g

97. Coconut Shrimp

Preparation Time: 9 minutes

Cooking Time: 31 minutes

Servings: 4

Ingredients:

- ½ cup pork rinds (crushed)
- 4 cups jumbo shrimp (deveined)
- ½ cup coconut flakes preferably
- 2 eggs
- ½ cup flour of coconut
- Any oil of your choice for frying at least half-inch in a pan
- Pepper & salt to taste

Dipping sauce:

- 2 to 3 tbsp powdered sugar as a substitute
- 3 tbsp mayonnaise
- ½ cup sour cream
- ¼ tsp coconut extract, or to taste
- 3 tbsp coconut cream
- ¼ tsp pineapple flavoring, or to taste
- 3 tbsp coconut flakes preferably unsweetened, this is optional

Directions:

Sauce:

1. Mix all ingredients into a tiny bowl for dipping sauce (Piña colada flavor). Combine well and put in the fridge until ready to serve.

Shrimps:

2. Whip eggs in a deep bowl, and in a small shallow bowl, add crushed pork rinds, coconut flour, sea salt, coconut flakes, and freshly ground black pepper.
3. Put shrimp one by one in mixed eggs for dipping, then in the coconut flour blend. Put them in your air fryer's basket.
4. Place shrimp battered in a single layer on your air fryer basket. Spritz shrimp with oil and cook for 8 to 10 minutes at 360°F, flipping them through halfway.
5. Enjoy hot with dipping sauce.

Nutrition:

- **Calories:** 340
- **Carbohydrates:** 9 g
- **Protein:** 25 g
- **Fat:** 16 g

98. Crispy Fish Sticks in Air Fryer

Preparation Time: 9 minutes

Cooking Time: 16 minutes

Servings: 4

Ingredients:

- 1 lb whitefish such as cod
- ¼ cup mayonnaise
- 2 tbsp Dijon mustard
- 2 tbsp water
- 1 ½ cup pork rind
- ¾ tsp Cajun seasoning
- Kosher salt & pepper, to taste

Directions:

1. Spray non-stick cooking spray on the air fryer rack.
2. Pat fish dry & cut into sticks about 1 inch by 2 inches broad
3. Stir together mayo, mustard, and water in a tiny small dish. Mix pork rinds & Cajun seasoning into another small container.
4. Adding kosher salt and pepper to taste (both pork rinds & seasoning can have a decent amount of kosher salt, so you can dip a finger to see how salty it is).
5. Dip fish sticks to cover in mayo mix & then tap off excess. Dip into the mixture of pork rind, then flip to cover. Place on the rack of an air fryer.
6. Set at 400°F to Air Fry & bake for 5 minutes, then turn fish with tongs and bake for another 5 minutes. Serve.

Nutrition:

- **Calories:** 263
- **Carbohydrates:** 1 g
- **Fat:** 16 g

- **Protein:** 26.4 g

99. Honey-Glazed Salmon

Preparation Time: 11 minutes

Cooking Time: 16 minutes

Servings: 2

Ingredients:

- 6 tsp gluten-free soy sauce
- 2 pieces of salmon fillets
- 3 tsp sweet rice wine
- 1 tsp water
- 6 tbsp honey

Directions:

1. Mix sweet rice wine, soy sauce, honey, and water.
2. Set half of it aside.
3. In half of it, marinate the fish and let it rest for 2 hours.
4. Let the air fryer preheat to 180°C.
5. Cook fish for 8 minutes, flip halfway through and cook for another 5 minutes.
6. Baste salmon with marinade mixture after 3 or 4 minutes.
7. Cook half of the marinade, reduce to half and serve with sauce.

Nutrition:

- **Calories:** 254
- **Carbohydrates:** 9.9 g
- **Fat:** 12 g
- **Protein:** 20 g

100. Basil-Parmesan Crusted Salmon

Preparation Time: 5 minutes

Cooking Time: 16 minutes

Servings: 4

Ingredients:

- 3 tbsp grated parmesan
- 4 skinless salmon fillets
- ¼ tsp salt and pepper
- 3 tbsp low-fat mayonnaise
- Basil leaves, chopped

- ½ lemon
- Olive oil

Directions:

1. Let the air fryer preheat to 400°F. Spray the basket with olive oil.
2. Season salmon with salt, pepper, and lemon juice.
3. Mix 2 tbsp parmesan cheese in a bowl with mayonnaise and basil leaves.
4. Add mixture and more parmesan on top of the salmon and cook for 7 minutes.
5. Serve hot.

Nutrition:

- **Calories:** 289
- **Carbohydrates:** 1.5 g
- **Protein:** 30 g
- **Fat:** 18.5 g

101. Cajun Shrimp in Air Fryer

Preparation Time: 9 minutes

Cooking Time: 22 minutes

Servings: 4

Ingredients:

- Peeled, 24 extra-jumbo shrimp
- 2 tbsp olive oil
- 1 tbsp Cajun seasoning
- 1 zucchini, thick slices (half-moons)
- ¼ cup cooked turkey
- Yellow squash, sliced half-moons
- ¼ tsp kosher salt:

Directions:

1. In a bowl, mix shrimp with Cajun seasoning.
2. Add zucchini, turkey, salt, squash, and coat with oil in another bowl.
3. Let the air fryer preheat to 400°F
4. Move shrimp and vegetable mix to fryer basket and cook for 3 minutes.
5. Serve hot.

Nutrition:

- **Calories:** 284
- **Carbohydrates:** 8 g

- **Protein:** 31 g
- **Fat:** 14 g

102. Crispy Air Fryer Fish

Preparation Time: 11 minutes

Cooking Time: 18 minutes

Servings: 4

Ingredients:

- 2 tsp old bay
- 4-6, cut in half, whiting fish fillets
- ¾ cup fine cornmeal
- ¼ cup flour
- 1 tsp paprika
- ½ tsp garlic powder
- 1 ½ tsp salt
- ½ tsp freshly ground black pepper

Directions:

1. In a zip lock bag, add all ingredients and coat fish fillets with it.
2. Spray oil on the air fryer basket and put fish in it.
3. Cook for 10 minutes at 400°F.
4. Serve with salad green.

Nutrition:

- **Calories:** 254
- **Carbohydrates:** 8.2 g
- **Fat:** 12.7 g
- **Protein:** 17.5 g

103. Air Fryer Lemon Cod

Preparation Time: 5 minutes

Cooking Time: 18 minutes

Servings: 1

Ingredients:

- 1 cod fillet
- Dried parsley, to taste
- Salt and pepper, to taste
- Garlic powder, to taste
- 1 lemon

Directions:

1. Mix all ingredients and coat the fish fillet with spices.
2. Slice the lemon and lay it at the bottom of the air fryer basket.
3. Put spiced fish on top. Cover fish with lemon slices.
4. Cook for ten minutes at 375°F, the internal temperature of the fish should be 145°F.
5. Serve.

Nutrition:

- **Calories:** 101
- **Carbohydrates:** 10 g
- **Protein:** 16 g
- **Fat:** 1 g

104. Air Fryer Salmon Fillets

Preparation Time: 5 minutes

Cooking Time: 16 minutes

Servings: 2

Ingredients:

- ¼ cup low-fat Greek yogurt:
- 2 salmon fillets
- 1 tbsp fresh dill (chopped)
- 1 lemon and lemon juice
- ½ tsp garlic powder
- Salt and pepper

Directions:

1. Cut the lemon into slices and lay them at the bottom of the air fryer basket.
2. Season salmon with salt and pepper. Put salmon on top of lemons.
3. Let it cook at 330°F for 15 minutes.
4. In the meantime, mix garlic powder, lemon juice, salt, and pepper with yogurt and dill.
5. Serve fish with sauce.

Nutrition:

- **Calories:** 194
- **Carbohydrates:** 6 g
- **Protein:** 25 g
- **Fat:** 7 g

105. Tuna Sandwich

Preparation Time: 9 minutes

Cooking Time: 25 minutes

Servings: 2

Ingredients:

- 1 5-oz can of white tuna in water
- 2 slices of wheat bread
- 1 tsp onion, chopped finely
- 1 celery stalk, chopped finely
- 2 tbsp mayonnaise, low fat
- 4 slices of ripe tomato
- ½ cup sharp cheddar cheese, reduced fat, shredded
- $^1/_8$ tsp celery salt
- Pinch of black pepper

Directions:

1. Put bread slices in the cooking basket. Set the fryer to 400°F and cook for 3 minutes.
2. Mix mayonnaise, tuna, salt, pepper, onion, and celery in a bowl. Divide mixture and spread in 2 toasted bread slices. Put 2 slices of tomato and cheese on top of each bread slice. Put one sandwich in the cooking basket at a time.
3. Set the fryer to 400°F and cook for 4 minutes. Cook another sandwich.

Nutrition:

- **Calories:** 160
- **Carbohydrates:** 14 g
- **Fat:** 10 g
- **Protein:** 24 g

106. Scrambled Salmon Egg

Preparation Time: 6 minutes

Cooking Time: 22 minutes

Servings: 2

Ingredients:

- 2 eggs
- 1 piece of smoked salmon
- 1 small red onion
- 2 tsp olive oil

- $1/3$ cup milk, low-fat
- $1/4$ tsp black pepper
- 2 tbsp fresh dill

Directions:

1. Preheat Air Fryer to 330°F.
2. In a skillet, heat oil. Sauté onions until translucent. Set aside.
3. Meanwhile, in a bowl, combine milk, eggs, salmon, and pepper.
4. Place the salmon mixture inside the basket. Scramble eggs until set.
5. Sprinkle dill all over. Serve.

Nutrition:

- **Calories:** 120
- **Carbohydrates:** 13 g
- **Fat:** 4.5 g
- **Protein:** 9.9 g

107.   Air Fryer Fish & Chips

Preparation Time: 11 minutes

Cooking Time: 38 minutes

Servings: 4

Ingredients:

- 4 cups of any fish fillet
- $1/4$ cup flour
- 1 cup whole wheat breadcrumbs
- 1 egg
- 2 tbsp oil
- 2 Potatoes
- 1 tsp salt
- 1 tsp tartar salt
- 4 oz salad green

Directions:

1. Cut potatoes in fries. Then coat with oil and salt.
2. Cook in the air fryer for 20 minutes at 400°F, and toss fries halfway through.
3. In the meantime, coat the fish in flour, then in whisked egg, and finally in breadcrumbs mix.
4. Place fish in the air fryer and let it cook at 330°F for 15 minutes.
5. Flip it halfway through, if needed.

6. Serve with tartar sauce and salad green.

Nutrition:

- **Calories:** 409
- **Carbohydrates:** 44 g
- **Protein:** 30 g
- **Fat:** 11 g

108.   Grilled Salmon with Lemon

Preparation Time: 9 minutes

Cooking Time: 22 minutes

Servings: 4

Ingredients:

- 2 tbsp olive oil
- 2 salmon fillets
- Lemon juice
- $1/3$ cup water
- $1/3$ cup gluten-free light soy sauce
- $1/3$ cup honey
- Scallion slices
- Cherry tomato
- Freshly ground black pepper, salt to taste

Directions:

1. Season salmon with pepper and salt
2. Mix tomato, honey, soy sauce, lemon juice, water, and oil in a bowl. Add salmon to this marinade and let it rest for at least 2 hours.
3. Let the air fryer preheat to 180°C.
4. Place fish in the air fryer and cook for 8 minutes.
5. Move to a dish and top with scallion slices.

Nutrition:

- **Calories:** 211
- **Carbohydrates:** 4.9 g
- **Fat:** 9 g
- **Protein:** 15 g

109.   Air-Fried Fish Nuggets

Preparation Time: 15 minutes

Cooking Time: 9 minutes

Servings: 4

Ingredients:

- 2 cups fish fillets in cubes (skinless)
- 1 egg, beaten
- 5 tbsp flour
- 5 tbsp water
- Salt and pepper to taste
- Breadcrumbs mix
- 1 tbsp smoked paprika
- ¼ cup whole wheat breadcrumbs:

Directions:

1. Season fish cubes with salt and pepper.
2. In a bowl, add flour and gradually add water, mixing as you add.
3. Then mix in the egg. And keep mixing but do not over-mix.
4. Coat cubes in batter, then in the breadcrumb mix. Coat well
5. Place cubes in a baking tray and spray with oil.
6. Let the air fryer preheat to 200°C.
7. Place cubes in the air fryer and cook for 12 minutes or until they are well-cooked and golden brown.
8. Serve with salad greens.

Nutrition:

- **Calories:** 184
- **Carbohydrates:** 10 g
- **Protein:** 19 g
- **Fat:** 3 g

110. Garlic Rosemary Grilled Prawns

Preparation Time: 5 minutes

Cooking Time: 11 minutes

Servings: 2

Ingredients:

- ½ tbsp Melted butter:
- Slices of green capsicum
- 8 prawns
- Rosemary leaves
- Kosher salt and pepper
- 3 to 4 cloves of minced garlic

Directions:

1. Mix all ingredients and marinate prawns in it for at least 60 minutes or more
2. Add 2 prawns and 2 slices of capsicum to each skewer.
3. Let the air fryer preheat to 180°C.
4. Cook for 5 to 6 minutes. Then change the temperature to 200°C and cook for another minute.
5. Serve with lemon wedges.

Nutrition:

- **Calories:** 194
- **Carbohydrates:** 12 g
- **Fat:** 10 g
- **Protein:** 26 g

111. Air-Fried Crumbed Fish

Preparation Time: 10 minutes

Cooking Time: 12 minutes

Servings: 2

Ingredients:

- 4 fish fillets
- 4 tbsp olive oil
- 1 egg beaten
- ¼ cup whole wheat breadcrumbs
- Lemon

Directions:

1. Let the air fryer preheat to 180°C.
2. In a bowl, mix breadcrumbs with oil. Mix well
3. First, coat the fish in egg mix (egg mix with water) and then in the breadcrumb mix. Coat well
4. Place in the air fryer, and let it cook for 10 to 12 minutes.
5. Serve hot with salad green and lemon.

Nutrition:

- **Calories:** 254
- **Carbohydrates:** 10.2 g
- **Fat:** 12.7 g
- **Protein:** 15.5 g

112. Parmesan Garlic Crusted Salmon

Preparation Time: 5 minutes

Cooking Time: 18 minutes

Servings: 2

Ingredients:

- ¼ cup whole wheat breadcrumbs
- 4 cups salmon
- 2 tbsp butter, melted
- ¼ tsp salt and pepper
- ¼ cup parmesan cheese (grated)
- 2 tsp minced garlic
- ½ tsp Italian seasoning

Directions:

1. Let the air fryer preheat to 400°F, and spray oil over the air fryer basket.
2. Pat dry salmon. In a bowl, mix parmesan cheese, Italian seasoning, and breadcrumbs. Mix melted butter with garlic in another pan and add to the breadcrumbs mix. Mix well.
3. Add salt and pepper to the salmon. On top of every salmon piece, add crust mix and press gently.
4. Let the air fryer preheat to 400°F and add salmon to it. Cook until done to your liking.
5. Serve hot with vegetable side dishes.

Nutrition:

- **Calories:** 330
- **Carbohydrates:** 11 g
- **Fat:** 19 g
- **Protein:** 31 g

113. Air Fryer Salmon with Maple Soy Glaze

Preparation Time: 5 minutes

Cooking Time: 8 minutes

Servings: 4

Ingredients:

- 3 tbsp pure maple syrup
- 3 tbsp gluten-free soy sauce
- 1 tbsp sriracha hot sauce
- 1 clove of minced garlic
- 4 salmon fillets, skinless

Directions:

1. Mix the sriracha, maple syrup, garlic, and soy sauce with salmon in a zip-lock bag.
2. Mix well and let it marinate for half an hour.
3. Let the air fryer preheat to 400°F with the oil spray basket.
4. Take the fish out from the marinade and pat dry.
5. Put salmon in the air fryer and cook for 7 to 8 minutes, or longer.
6. In the meantime, in a saucepan, add marinade, and let it simmer until reduced to half.
7. Add glaze over salmon and serve.

Nutrition:

- **Calories:** 292
- **Carbohydrates:** 12 g
- **Protein:** 35 g
- **Fat:** 11 g

114. Air Fried Cajun Salmon

Preparation Time: 9 minutes

Cooking Time: 22 minutes

Servings: 1

Ingredients:

- 1 piece of fresh salmon
- 2 tbsp Cajun seasoning
- Lemon juice

Directions:

1. Let the air fryer preheat to 180° C.
2. Pat dry salmon fillet. Rub lemon juice and Cajun seasoning over the fish fillet.
3. Place in the air fryer, and cook for 7 minutes. Serve with salad greens and lime wedges.

Nutrition:

- **Calories:** 216
- **Carbohydrates:** 5.6 g
- **Fat:** 19 g

- **Protein:** 19.2 g

115.   Air Fryer Shrimp Scampi

Preparation Time: 5 minutes

Cooking Time: 11 minutes

Servings: 2

Ingredients:

- 4 cups raw shrimp
- 1 tbsp lemon juice
- Chopped fresh basil
- 2 tsp red pepper flakes
- 2 ½ tbsp butter
- Chopped chives
- 2 tbsp chicken stock
- 1 tbsp minced garlic

Directions:

- Let the air fryer preheat with a metal pan to 330°F
- Add garlic, red pepper flakes, and half of the butter in a hot pan. Let it cook for 2 minutes.
- Add butter, shrimp, chicken stock, minced garlic, chives, lemon juice, and basil to the pan. Let it cook for 5 minutes.
- Take it out from the air fryer and let it rest for 1 minute.
- Add fresh basil leaves and chives and serve.

Nutrition:

- **Calories:** 287
- **Carbohydrates:** 7.5 g
- **Fat:** 5.5 g
- **Protein:** 18 g

116.   Sesame Seeds Fish Fillet

Preparation Time: 11 minutes

Cooking Time: 23 minutes

Servings: 2

Ingredients:

- 3 tbsp plain flour
- 1 egg, beaten
- 5 frozen fish fillets

For coating:

- 2 tbsp oil
- ½ cup sesame seeds
- Rosemary herbs
- 5 to 6 biscuit crumbs
- Kosher salt& pepper, to taste

Directions:

1. For 2 minutes, sauté sesame seeds in a pan, without oil. Brown them and set them aside.
2. On a plate, mix all coating ingredients
3. Place aluminum foil on the air fryer basket and let it preheat to 200°C.
4. First, coat the fish in flour. Then in egg, then in coating mix.
5. Place in the Air fryer. If fillets are frozen, cook for 10 minutes, then turn the fillet and cook for another 4 minutes.
6. If not frozen, then cook for 8 minutes and 2 minutes.

Nutrition:

- **Calories:** 250
- **Carbohydrates:** 12.4 g
- **Fat:** 8 g
- **Protein:** 20 g

117.   Lemon Pepper Shrimp in Air Fryer

Preparation Time: 5 minutes

Cooking Time: 11 minutes

Servings: 2

Ingredients:

- 1 ½ cup peeled raw shrimp, deveined
- ½ tbsp olive oil
- ¼ tsp garlic powder
- 1 tsp lemon pepper
- ¼ tsp paprika
- Juice of one lemon

Directions:

1. Let the air fryer preheat to 400°F
2. Mix lemon pepper, olive oil, paprika, garlic powder, and lemon juice in a bowl. Mix well. Add the shrimp and coat well
3. Add the shrimp to the air fryer, cook for 6 to 8 minutes and top with lemon slices and serve

Nutrition:

- **Calories:** 237
- **Carbohydrates:** 11 g
- **Fat:** 6 g
- **Protein:** 36 g

118.   Air Fried Fish and Chips

Preparation Time: 15 minutes

Cooking Time: 31 minutes

Servings: 4

Ingredients:

- Cooking spray
- 4 skinless tilapia fillets
- 2 tbsp water
- 2 russet potatoes, scrubbed
- 2 large eggs
- ½ cup malt vinegar
- 1 cup whole-wheat panko (Japanese-style breadcrumbs)
- 1 cup all-purpose flour
- 1 ¼ tsp kosher salt, divided

Directions:

1. You need to cut potatoes into spirals and cook them in batches for them to come out very crispy. So, place the first batch in your air fryer basket. Spray them with cooking spray. Toss them for even coating.
2. Cook potatoes for 10 minutes at 375°F. Don't forget to turn them over after 5 minutes. After 10 minutes, they should be crispy and golden brown in color. Remove them and put them in an airtight container

to keep them warm. Then you can cook the next batch.

3. When you have been able to cook them all, you can sprinkle ¼ tsp salt on them.
4. Mix ½ tsp salt with flour and stir them together.
5. Whisk eggs together with some water in another bowl. Also, mix the remaining salt with panko in a third bowl.
6. Cut each fish fillet into 2 long strips and toss them in the flour mixture. After that, you can now dip coated fillets in an egg mixture. Finally, dredge them in a panko mixture. Try to spray both sides of each fish fillet with cooking spray.
7. Now, it is time to cook fish too. Place them on a single layer in your air fryer basket. Cook them at 375°F for 10 minutes.
8. When they are done, you can serve fish along with potato spirals and 2 tbsp malt vinegar.

Nutrition:

- **Calories:** 415
- **Carbohydrates:** 46 g
- **Protein:** 44 g
- **Fat:** 7 g

119.   Scallops and Dill

Preparation Time: 5 minutes

Cooking Time: 11 minutes

Servings: 4

Ingredients:

- 1 lb sea scallops
- 1 tbsp lemon juice
- 1 tsp dill
- 2 tsp olive oil
- Black pepper and salt

Directions:

1. Mix scallops with oil, dill, pepper, lemon juice, and salt in the air fryer. Cook for 5 minutes at 360°F.
2. Dispose of the uncovered ones. Divide dill sauce and scallops on plates. Serve.

Nutrition:

- **Calories:** 451
- **Carbohydrates:** 3 g
- **Fat:** 39 g
- **Protein:** 19 g

120.   Crispy Fish Sandwiches

Preparation Time: 10 minutes

Cooking Time: 10 minutes

Servings: 2

Ingredients:

- 2 cod fillets
- 2 tbsp all-purpose flour
- ¼ tsp pepper
- 1 tbsp lemon juice
- ¼ tsp salt
- ½ tsp garlic powder
- 1 egg
- ½ tbsp mayo
- ½ cup whole wheat breadcrumbs

Directions:

1. Add salt, flour, pepper, and garlic powder in a bowl.
2. In a separate bowl, add lemon juice, mayo, and egg.
3. In another bowl, add breadcrumbs.
4. Coat fish in flour, then in egg, then in breadcrumbs.
5. With cooking oil, spray the basket and put the fish in the basket. Also, spray fish with cooking oil.
6. Cook at 400⁰ F for 10 minutes. This fish is soft, be careful when you flip it.

Nutrition:

- **Calories:** 218
- **Net Carbohydrates:** 7 g
- **Fat:** 12 g
- **Protein:** 22 g

121.   Lean Pork and Shrimp Dumplings

Preparation Time: 9 minutes

Cooking Time: 21 minutes

Servings: 4

Ingredients:

- 12 thin wonton wrappers, separated

Filling:

- ½ cup lean ground pork
- ½ cup peeled shrimp, uncooked, chopped
- ⅛ cup carrots, diced
- ⅛ cup jicama, diced
- ⅛ cup chives, chopped roughly
- ⅛ tsp rice wine
- ⅛ tsp salt
- 1/16 tsp black pepper

Sauce:

- 2 tbsp light soy sauce
- 1 tbsp lime juice, freshly squeezed
- ¼ tsp roasted sesame oil
- ⅛ tsp stevia

Directions:

1. Preheat Air Fryer to 300°F.
2. To make dumplings, combine filling ingredients in a food processor. Process until the mixture looks like a coarse paste. Rest for 5 minutes before wrapping.
3. Drape dumpling wrapper. Scoop in ½ tbsp filling. Moisten the edges of the wrapper with water.
4. Gently press down on the filling until the dumpling gently slides between your fingers and into your palm. Squeeze in dumpling sides, but leave the top open. Gently tap dumplings on a flat surface to make the base even. Continue pinching and tapping until the dumpling can stand on its own. Place on a baking sheet lined with parchment paper. Repeat the step for all fillings and wrappers. Freeze for at least ½ hour before frying. Do not thaw.

5. Place into Air Fryer basket. Cook for 15 minutes, or until wrappers turn golden brown, and tops are set. Remove from the basket.
6. For the sauce, pour the ingredients into a bowl. Stir until sugar dissolves.
7. Serve equal portions on plates with a small amount of sauce on the side.

Nutrition:

- **Calories:** 180
- **Carbohydrates:** 20 g
- **Fat:** 6 g
- **Protein:** 10 g

Chapter 7. Meat Recipes

122. Air Fryer Steak

Preparation Time: 6 minutes

Cooking Time: 15 minutes

Servings: 2

Ingredients:

- 1 rib-eye steak or New York City strip steak
- ½ tsp Salt and pepper
- 1 tsp Garlic powder
- ½ tsp Paprika
- 1 tsp Butter
- Olive oil

Directions:

1. Place meat to sit in a bowl at room temperature level.
2. Spray olive oil onto both sides of the steak.
3. Add salt and pepper to season.
4. Add garlic powder and paprika to the mixture.
5. Adjust the temperature of the air fryer to 400°F.
6. Place steak in the fryer, and cook for 12 minutes
7. Lead it with butter when ready, then serve.

Nutrition:

- **Calories:** 301
- **Carbohydrates:** 0 g
- **Fat:** 23 g
- **Protein:** 23 g

123. Pork on a Blanket

Preparation Time: 12 minutes

Cooking Time: 18 minutes

Servings: 4

Ingredients:

- ½ puff defrosted pastry sheet
- 16 thick smoked sausages
- 15 ml milk

Directions:

1. Adjust the temperature of the air fryer to 200° C and set the timer to 5 minutes.
2. Cut puff pastry into 64 x 38 mm strips.
3. Place a cocktail sausage at the end of the puff pastry and roll around the sausage, sealing the dough with some water.
4. Brush the top of the sausages wrapped in milk and place them in the preheated air fryer.
5. Cook at 200°C for 10 minutes or until golden brown.

Nutrition:

- **Calories:** 242
- **Carbohydrates:** 0 g
- **Fat:** 14 g
- **Protein:** 27 g

124. Vietnamese Grilled Pork

Preparation Time: 6 minutes

Cooking Time: 16 minutes

Servings: 6

Ingredients:

- 1 lb sliced pork shoulder, pastured, fat trimmed

For marinade:

- ¼ cup minced white onions
- 1 tbsp minced garlic
- 1 tbsp lemongrass paste
- 1 tbsp erythritol sweetener
- ½ tsp pepper
- 1 tbsp fish sauce
- 2 tsp soy sauce
- 2 tbsp olive oil

Directions:

1. Combine all marinade ingredients for the marinade.
2. Cut pork into ½-inch slices, cut each slice into 1-inches pieces, then add them into the plastic bag containing marinade, seal the bag, turn it upside down to coat pork pieces with marinade and marinate for a minimum of 1 hour.
3. Then switch on the air fryer, insert the fryer basket, grease it with olive oil, then shut its lid, set the fryer at 400°F, and preheat for 5 minutes.
4. Open the fryer, add marinated pork in it in a single layer, close with its lid and cook for 10 minutes until nicely golden and cooked, flipping the pork halfway through frying.
5. When the air fryer beeps, open its lid, transfer pork onto a serving plate, and keep warm.
6. Air fryer the remaining pork pieces in the same manner and then serve.

Nutrition:

- **Calories:** 231
- **Carbohydrates:** 4 g
- **Fat:** 16 g
- **Protein:** 16 g

125.   Provencal Ribs

Preparation Time: 6 minutes

Cooking Time: 80 minutes

Servings: 4

Ingredients:

- 500 g pork ribs
- ½ cup Provencal herbs
- ½ tsp Salt
- 1 tbsp Ground pepper
- 2 tbsp Oil

Directions:

1. Put ribs in a bowl and add some oil, Provencal herbs, salt, and ground pepper.
2. Stir well and leave in the fridge for at least 1 hour.
3. Put ribs in the basket of the air fryer and select 200°C for 20 minutes.
4. From time to time, shake the basket and remove the ribs.

Nutrition:

- **Calories:** 296
- **Carbohydrates:** 0 g
- **Fat:** 22.63 g
- **Protein:** 21.71 g

126.   Air Fryer Beef Steak Kabobs with Vegetables

Preparation Time: 9 minutes

Cooking Time: 11 minutes

Servings: 4

Ingredients:

- 2 tbsp light soy sauce
- 4 cups lean beef chuck ribs, cut into one-inch pieces
- $1/3$ cup low-fat sour cream
- ½ onion
- 6-inch skewers (8)
- 1 bell peppers

Directions:

1. Add soy sauce and sour cream in a mixing bowl, and mix well. Add lean beef chunks, coat well, and let it marinate for half an hour or more.

2. Cut onion and bell pepper into one-inch pieces. In water, soak skewers for 10 minutes.
3. Add onions, bell peppers, and beef on skewers; alternatively, sprinkle with black pepper.
4. Let it cook for 10 minutes in a preheated air fryer at 400°F, and flip halfway through.
5. Serve with yogurt dipping sauce.

Nutrition:

- **Calories:** 268
- **Carbohydrates:** 15 g
- **Protein:** 20 g
- **Fat:** 10 g

127. Fried Pork Chops

Preparation Time: 9 minutes

Cooking Time: 38 minutes

Servings: 2

Ingredients:

- 3 cloves of ground garlic
- 2 tbsp olive oil
- 1 tbsp marinade
- 4 thawed pork chops

Directions:

1. Mix cloves of ground garlic, oil, and marinade in a bowl.
2. Apply the mixture to the pork chops.
3. Put chops in the air fryer and cook at 360°C for 35 minutes.

Nutrition:

- **Calories:** 118
- **Carbohydrates:** 0 g
- **Fat:** 6.85 g
- **Protein:** 13.12 g

128. Pork Liver

Preparation Time: 9 minutes

Cooking Time: 16 minutes

Servings: 4

Ingredients:

- 500 g pork liver cut into steaks
- 4 oz. Breadcrumbs
- ½ tsp Salt
- 2 tbsp Ground pepper
- 1 lemon
- ½ cup Extra virgin olive oil

Directions:

1. Put steaks on a plate or bowl.
2. Add lemon juice, salt, and ground pepper.
3. Leave a few minutes to macerate pork liver fillets.
4. Drain well and go through breadcrumbs, it is not necessary to pass fillets through the beaten egg because the liver is very moist, and the breadcrumbs are perfectly glued.
5. Spray with extra virgin olive oil. If you don't have a sprayer, paint with a silicone brush.
6. Put pork liver fillets in the air fryer basket.
7. Program 180°C, 10 minutes.
8. Take out if you see them golden to your liking and put another batch.
9. You should not pile pork liver fillets, which are well extended so that empanada is crispy on all sides.

Nutrition:

- **Calories:** 120
- **Carbohydrates:** 0 g
- **Fat:** 3.41 g
- **Protein:** 20.99 g

129. Air Fried Meatloaf

Preparation Time: 6 minutes

Cooking Time: 22 minutes

Servings: 2

Ingredients:

- ½ lb ground beef
- ½ lb ground turkey
- 1 onion, chopped
- ¼ cup panko bread crumbs
- 3 tbsp ketchup
- ¼ cup brown sugar
- 1 egg, beaten

- Salt and pepper to taste

Directions:

1. Preheat the air fryer to 400°F.
2. Let ground beef and ground turkey sit on the counter for 10 to 15 minutes, as it will be easier to hand mix without being chilled from the refrigerator.
3. Combine all ingredients.
4. Form into a loaf in a dish and place the dish in a frying basket. Spritz the top with a little olive oil.
5. Bake for 25 minutes, or until browned. Let settle for about 10 minutes before serving.

Nutrition:

- **Calories:** 381
- **Carbohydrates:** 9.6 g
- **Fat:** 5 g
- **Protein:** 38 g

130.   Pork Tenderloin

Preparation Time: 9 minutes

Cooking Time: 33 minutes

Servings: 6

Ingredients:

- 1 ½ lb pork tenderloin

Directions:

1. Adjust the temperature of the Air Fryer to 370°F.
2. Lay pork in the Air Fryer basket.
3. Cook at 400°F for about 30 minutes, turning halfway through cooking time for a proper cook.
4. Serve.

Nutrition:

- **Calories:** 419
- **Carbohydrates:** 0 g
- **Fat:** 3.5 g
- **Protein:** 26 g

131.   Pork Bondiola Chop

Preparation Time: 8 minutes

Cooking Time: 22 minutes

Servings: 4

Ingredients:

- 1 kg bondiola, in pieces
- Breadcrumbs, as needed
- 2 beaten eggs
- Seasoning, to taste

Directions:

1. Cut the bondiola into small pieces
2. Add seasonings to taste.
3. Pour beaten eggs on seasoned bondiola.
4. Add breadcrumbs.
5. Cook in the air fryer for 20 minutes while turning the food halfway.
6. Serve

Nutrition:

- **Calories:** 265
- **Carbohydrates:** 0 g
- **Fat:** 20.36 g
- **Protein:** 19.14 g

132.   Mustard Lamb Loin Chops

Preparation Time: 15 minutes

Cooking Time: 30 minutes

Servings: 4

Ingredients:

- 8: 4-oz lamb loin chops
- 2 tbsp Dijon mustard
- 1 tbsp fresh lemon juice
- ½ tsp olive oil
- 1 tsp dried tarragon
- Salt and black pepper, to taste

Directions:

1. Preheat the Air fryer to 390°F and grease an Air fryer basket.
2. Mix mustard, lemon juice, oil, tarragon, salt, and black pepper in a large bowl.
3. Coat chops generously with mustard mixture and arrange in the Air fryer basket.

4. Cook for about 15 minutes, flipping once in between, and dish out to serve hot.

Nutrition:

- **Calories:** 433
- **Carbohydrates:** 0.6 g
- **Fat:** 17.6 g
- **Protein:** 64.1 g

133.   Herbed Lamb Chops

Preparation Time: 10 minutes

Cooking Time: 7 minutes

Servings: 2

Ingredients:

- 4 4-oz lamb chops
- 1 tbsp fresh lemon juice
- 1 tbsp olive oil
- 1 tsp dried rosemary
- 1 tsp dried thyme
- 1 tsp dried oregano
- ½ tsp ground cumin
- ½ tsp ground coriander
- Salt and black pepper, to taste

Directions:

1. Preheat the Air fryer to 390°F and grease an Air fryer basket.
2. Mix the lemon juice, oil, herbs, and spices in a large bowl.
3. Coat chops generously with herb mixture and refrigerate to marinate for about 1 hour.
4. Arrange chops in the Air fryer basket and cook for about 7 minutes, flipping once in between.
5. Dish out lamb chops on a platter and serve hot.

Nutrition:

- **Calories:** 491
- **Carbohydrates:** 1.6 g
- **Fat:** 24 g
- **Protein:** 64 g

134.   Za'atar Lamb Loin Chops

Preparation Time: 10 minutes

Cooking Time: 30 minutes

Servings: 4

Ingredients:

- 3 ½-oz bone-in lamb loin chops (8), trimmed
- 3 garlic cloves, crushed
- 1 tbsp fresh lemon juice
- 1 tsp olive oil
- 1 tbsp Za'atar
- Salt and black pepper, to taste

Directions:

1. Preheat the Air fryer to 400°F and grease an Air fryer basket.
2. Mix garlic, lemon juice, oil, Za'atar, salt, and black pepper in a large bowl.
3. Coat chops generously with herb mixture and arrange chops in the Air fryer basket.
4. Cook for about 15 minutes, flipping twice in between, and dish out lamb chops to serve hot.

Nutrition:

- **Calories:** 433
- **Carbohydrates:** 0.6 g
- **Fat:** 17.6 g
- **Protein:** 64.1 g

135.   Pesto Coated Rack of Lamb

Preparation Time: 15 minutes

Cooking Time: 15 minutes

Servings: 4

Ingredients:

- ½ bunch of fresh mint
- 1 ½ lb rack of lamb (1)
- 1 garlic clove
- ¼ cup extra-virgin olive oil
- ½ tbsp honey

- Salt and black pepper, to taste

Directions:

1. Preheat the Air fryer to 200°F and grease an Air fryer basket.
2. Put mint, garlic, oil, honey, salt, and black pepper in a blender and pulse until smooth to make pesto.
3. Coat the rack of lamb with this pesto on both sides and arrange it in the air fryer basket.
4. Cook for about 15 minutes and cut the rack into individual chops to serve.

Nutrition:

- **Calories:** 406
- **Carbohydrates:** 2.9 g
- **Fat:** 27.7 g
- **Protein:** 34.9 g

136.   Spiced Lamb Steaks

Preparation Time: 15 minutes

Cooking Time: 15 minutes

Servings: 3

Ingredients:

- ½ onion, roughly chopped
- 1 ½ lb boneless lamb sirloin steaks
- 5 garlic cloves, peeled
- 1 tbsp fresh ginger, peeled
- 1 tsp garam masala
- 1 tsp ground fennel
- ½ tsp ground cumin
- ½ tsp ground cinnamon
- ½ tsp cayenne pepper
- Salt and black pepper, to taste

Directions:

1. Preheat the Air fryer to 330°F and grease an Air fryer basket.
2. Put onion, garlic, ginger, and spices in a blender and pulse until smooth.
3. Coat lamb steaks with this mixture on both sides and refrigerate to marinate for about 24 hours.

4. Arrange lamb steaks in the Air fryer basket and cook for about 15 minutes, flipping once in between.
5. Dish out steaks on a platter and serve warm.

Nutrition:

- **Calories:** 252
- **Carbohydrates:** 4.2 g
- **Fat:** 16.7 g
- **Protein:** 21.7 g

137.   Steak

Preparation Time: 6 minutes

Cooking Time: 18 minutes

Servings: 2

Ingredients:

- 2 steaks, grass-fed, each about 6 oz and ¾ inch thick
- 1 tbsp butter, unsalted
- ¾ tsp pepper
- ½ tsp garlic powder
- ¾ tsp salt
- 1 tsp olive oil

Directions:

1. Switch on the air fryer, insert the fryer basket, grease it with olive oil, then shut its lid, set the fryer at 400°F, and preheat for 5 minutes.
2. Meanwhile, coat the steaks with oil and then season with black pepper, garlic, and salt.
3. Open the fryer, add steaks to it, close with its lid and cook 10 to 18 minutes until nicely golden and steaks are cooked to desired doneness, flipping steaks halfway through frying.
4. When the air fryer beeps, open its lid and transfer the steaks to a cutting board.
5. Take two large pieces of aluminum foil, place a steak on each piece, top the steak with ½ tbsp butter, then cover with foil and let it rest for 5 minutes.
6. Serve straight away.

Nutrition:

- **Calories:** 82
- **Carbohydrates:** 0 g
- **Fat:** 5 g
- **Protein:** 8.7 g

138. Marinated Loin Potatoes

Preparation Time: 8 minutes

Cooking Time: 61 minutes

Servings: 2

Ingredients:

- 2 medium potatoes
- 4 fillets of marinated loin
- A little extra virgin olive oil
- Salt, to taste

Directions:

1. Peel potatoes and cut. Cut with match-sized mandolin, potatoes with a cane but very thin.
2. Wash and immerse in water for 30 minutes.
3. Drain and dry well.
4. Add a little oil and stir so that oil permeates well in all potatoes.
5. Go to the basket of the air fryer and distribute well.
6. Cook at 160°C for 10 minutes.
7. Take out the basket and shake so that potatoes take off. Let potato tender. If it is not, leave 5 more minutes.
8. Place steaks on top of potatoes.
9. Select, 10 minutes, and 180°C for 5 minutes again.

Nutrition:

- **Calories:** 136
- **Carbohydrates:** 1.9 g
- **Fat:** 5.1 g
- **Protein:** 20.7 g

139. Beef with Mushrooms

Preparation Time: 8 minutes

Cooking Time: 41 minutes

Servings: 4

Ingredients:

- 300 g beef
- 150 g mushrooms
- 1 onion
- 1 tsp olive oil
- 100 g vegetable broth
- 1 tsp basil
- 1 tsp chili
- 30 g tomato juice

Directions:

1. For this recipe, you should take a solid piece of beef. Take the beef and pierce the meat with a knife.
2. Rub it with olive oil, basil, chili, and tomato juice.
3. Chop onion and mushrooms and pour them with vegetable broth.
4. Cook vegetables for 5 minutes.
5. Take a big tray and put meat in it. Add vegetable broth to the tray too. It will make meat juicy.
6. Preheat the air fryer oven to 180°C and cook it for 35 minutes.

Nutrition:

- **Calories:** 175
- **Carbohydrates:** 4.4 g
- **Protein:** 24.9 g
- **Fat:** 6.2 g

140. Cheesy and Crunchy Russian Steaks

Preparation Time: 6 minutes

Cooking Time: 22 minutes

Servings: 4

Ingredients:

- 800 g minced pork
- 200 g cream cheese
- 50 g peeled walnuts
- 1 onion

- Salt and ground pepper, to taste
- 1 egg
- Breadcrumbs, as needed
- Extra virgin olive oil

Directions:

1. Put onion cut into quarters in a thermo mix glass and select 5 seconds speed 5.
2. Add minced meat, cheese, egg, salt, and pepper.
3. Select 10 seconds, speed 5, and turn left.
4. Add chopped and peeled walnuts and select 4 seconds, turn left speed 5.
5. Pass dough to a bowl.
6. Make Russian steaks and go through breadcrumbs.
7. Paint Russian fillets with extra virgin olive oil on both sides with a brush.
8. Put in the basket of the air fryer, without stacking Russian fillets.
9. Select 180°C, 15 minutes.

Nutrition:

- **Calories:** 123.2
- **Carbohydrates:** 0 g
- **Fat:** 3.41 g
- **Protein:** 20.99 g

141. Roasted Vegetable and Chicken Salad

Preparation Time: 9 minutes

Cooking Time: 13 minutes

Servings: 4

Ingredients:

- 3 boneless, skinless chicken breasts
- 1 small red onion, sliced
- 1 orange bell pepper, sliced
- 1 cup sliced yellow summer squash
- 4 tbsp honey mustard salad dressing, divided
- ½ tsp dried thyme
- ½ cup mayonnaise
- 2 tbsp freshly squeezed lemon juice

Directions:

1. Place chicken, onion, pepper, and squash in the air fryer basket. Drizzle with 1 tbsp honey mustard salad dressing, add thyme and toss.
2. Roast at 400° F (204° C) for 10 to 13 minutes or until the chicken is 165° F (74° C) on a food thermometer, tossing food once during cooking time.
3. Transfer chicken and vegetables to a bowl and mix in the remaining 3 tbsp honey mustard salad dressing, mayonnaise, and lemon juice. Serve on lettuce leaves, if desired.

Nutrition:

- **Calories:** 495
- **Carbohydrates:** 18 g
- **Fat:** 23 g
- **Protein:** 51 g

142. Chicken Satay

Preparation Time: 12 minutes

Cooking Time: 18 minutes

Servings: 4

Ingredients:

- ½ cup crunchy peanut butter
- ⅓ cup chicken broth
- 3 tbsp low-sodium soy sauce
- 2 tbsp freshly squeezed lemon juice
- 2 cloves garlic, minced
- 2 tbsp olive oil
- 1 tsp curry powder
- 1 lb (454 g) chicken tenders

Directions:

1. In a medium bowl, combine peanut butter, chicken broth, soy sauce, lemon juice, garlic, olive oil, and curry powder, and mix well with a wire whisk until smooth. Remove 2 tbsp of this mixture to a small bowl. Put the remaining sauce into a serving bowl and set aside.
2. Add chicken tenders to a bowl with 2 tbsp sauce and stir to coat. Let stand for a few minutes to marinate, then run a bamboo

skewer through each chicken tender lengthwise.

3. Put chicken in the air fryer basket and air fry in batches at 390°F (199°C) for 6 to 9 minutes or until the chicken reaches 165°F (74°C) on a meat thermometer. Serve chicken with reserved sauce.

Nutrition:

- **Calories:** 449
- **Carbohydrates:** 8 g
- **Fat:** 28 g
- **Protein:** 46 g

143.   Mini Turkey Meatloaves

Preparation Time: 6 minutes

Cooking Time: 22 minutes

Servings: 4

Ingredients:

- $1/3$ cup minced onion
- ¼ cup grated carrot
- 2 garlic cloves, minced
- 2 tbsp ground almonds
- 2 tsp olive oil
- 1 tsp dried marjoram
- 1 egg white
- ¾ lb (340 g) ground turkey breast

Directions:

1. Stir onion, carrot, garlic, almonds, olive oil, marjoram, and egg white.
2. Add ground turkey. With your hands, gently but thoroughly mix until combined.
3. Double 16 foil muffin cup liners to make 8 cups. Divide the turkey mixture evenly among the liners.
4. Bake at 400°F (204°C) for 20 to 24 minutes, or until meatloaves reach an internal temperature of 165°F (74°C) on a meat thermometer. Serve immediately.

Nutrition:

- **Calories:** 142
- **Carbohydrates:** 3 g

- **Fat:** 5 g
- **Protein:** 23 g

144.   Chicken Fajitas with Avocados

Preparation Time: 9 minutes

Cooking Time: 14 minutes

Servings: 4

Ingredients:

- 4 boneless, skinless chicken breasts, sliced
- 1 small red onion, sliced
- 2 red bell peppers, sliced
- ½ cup spicy ranch salad dressing, divided
- ½ tsp dried oregano
- 8 corn tortillas
- 2 cups torn butter lettuce
- 2 avocados, peeled and chopped

Directions:

1. Place the chicken, onion, and pepper in an air fryer basket. Drizzle with 1 tbsp salad dressing and add oregano. Toss to combine.
2. Air fry at 380°F (193°C) for 10 to 14 minutes or until the chicken is 165°F (74°C) on a food thermometer.
3. Transfer chicken and vegetables to a bowl and toss with the remaining salad dressing.
4. Serve chicken mixture with tortillas, lettuce, and avocados, and let everyone make their own creations.

Nutrition:

- **Calories:** 784
- **Carbohydrates:** 39 g
- **Fat:** 38 g
- **Protein:** 72 g

145.   Crispy Buttermilk Fried Chicken

Preparation Time: 8 minutes

Cooking Time: 28 minutes

Servings: 4

Ingredients:

- 6 chicken pieces: drumsticks, breasts, and thighs
- 1 cup flour
- 2 tsp paprika
- Pinch salt
- Freshly pepper, to taste
- $^1/_3$ cup buttermilk
- 2 eggs
- 2 tbsp olive oil
- 1 ½ cups breadcrumbs

Directions:

1. Pat chicken dry. In a bowl, combine flour, paprika, salt, and pepper.
2. In another bowl, beat buttermilk with eggs until smooth.
3. In a third bowl, combine olive oil and bread crumbs until mixed.
4. Dredge chicken in flour, then into eggs to coat, and finally into breadcrumbs, patting crumbs firmly onto chicken skin.
5. Air fry chicken at 370°F (188°C) for 20 to 25 minutes, turning each piece over halfway during cooking until meat registers 165°F (74°C) on a meat thermometer and the chicken is brown and crisp. Let cool for 5 minutes, then serve.

Nutrition:

- **Calories:** 645
- **Carbohydrates:** 55 g
- **Fat:** 17 g
- **Protein:** 62 g

146. Garlicky Chicken with Creamer Potatoes

Preparation Time: 11 minutes

Cooking Time: 23 minutes

Servings: 4

Ingredients:

- 1 (2 ½- to 3-lb / 1.1- to 1.4-kg) broiler-fryer whole chicken
- 2 tbsp olive oil

- ½ tsp garlic salt
- 8 cloves garlic, peeled
- 1 slice lemon
- ½ tsp dried thyme
- ½ tsp dried marjoram
- 12 to 16 creamer potatoes, scrubbed

Directions:

1. Do not wash the chicken before cooking. Remove it from its packaging and pat the chicken dry.
2. Combine olive oil and salt in a small bowl. Rub half of this mixture on the inside of the chicken, under the skin, and on the chicken skin. Place garlic cloves and lemon slices inside the chicken. Sprinkle chicken with thyme and marjoram.
3. Put chicken in air fryer basket. Surround with potatoes and drizzle potatoes with the remaining olive oil mixture.
4. Roast at 380° F (193°C) for 25 minutes, then test the temperature of the chicken. It should be 160° F (71°C). Test at the thickest part of the breast, making sure the probe doesn't touch bone. If the chicken isn't done yet, return it to the air fryer and roast it for 4 to 5 minutes, or until the temperature is 160°F (71°C).
5. When the chicken is done, transfer it with the potatoes to a serving platter and cover it with foil.

Nutrition:

- **Calories:** 492
- **Carbohydrates:** 20 g
- **Fat:** 14 g
- **Protein:** 68 g

147. Baked Chicken Cordon Bleu

Preparation Time: 15 minutes

Cooking Time: 13 minutes

Servings: 4

Ingredients:

- 4 chicken breast fillets

- ¼ cup chopped ham
- ⅓ cup grated Swiss or Gruyere cheese
- ¼ cup flour
- A pinch salt
- Freshly pepper, to taste
- ½ tsp dried marjoram
- 1 egg
- 1 cup whole-wheat breadcrumbs
- Olive oil, for misting

Directions:

1. Put chicken breast fillets on a work surface and gently press them with the palm of your hand to make them a bit thinner. Don't tear meat.
2. In a small bowl, combine ham and cheese. Divide this mixture among chicken fillets. Wrap the chicken around the filling to enclose it, using toothpicks to hold the chicken together.
3. In a shallow bowl, mix flour, salt, pepper, and marjoram. In another bowl, beat the egg. Spread breadcrumbs out on a plate.
4. Dip chicken into the flour mixture, then into the egg, then into breadcrumbs to coat thoroughly.
5. Put the chicken in the air fryer basket and mist it with olive oil.
6. Bake at 380ºF (193ºC) for 13 to 15 minutes or until the chicken is thoroughly cooked to 165ºF (74ºC). Carefully remove toothpicks and serve.

Nutrition:

- **Calories:** 479
- **Carbohydrates:** 26 g
- **Fat:** 12 g
- **Protein:** 64 g

148. Chicken Tenders and Vegetables

Preparation Time: 9 minutes

Cooking Time: 18 minutes

Servings: 4

Ingredients:

- 1 lb (454 g) chicken tenders
- 1 tbsp honey
- Pinch salt
- Freshly pepper, to taste
- ½ cup soft fresh breadcrumbs
- ½ tsp dried thyme
- 1 tbsp olive oil
- 2 carrots, sliced
- 12 small red potatoes

Directions:

1. Toss chicken tenders with honey, salt, and pepper.
2. Mix in a shallow bowl with breadcrumbs, thyme, and olive oil; mix.
3. Coat tenders in breadcrumbs, pressing firmly onto the meat.
4. Place carrots and potatoes in the air fryer basket and top with chicken tenders.
5. Roast at 380ºF (193ºC) for 18 to 20 minutes or until the chicken is cooked to 165ºF (74ºC) and the vegetables are tender, shaking the basket halfway during cooking time.

Nutrition:

- **Calories:** 379
- **Carbohydrates:** 35 g
- **Fat:** 8 g
- **Protein:** 41 g

149. Greek Chicken Kebabs

Preparation Time: 15 minutes

Cooking Time: 16 minutes

Servings: 4

Ingredients:

- 3 tbsp freshly squeezed lemon juice
- 2 tsp olive oil
- 2 tbsp chopped fresh flat-leaf parsley
- ½ tsp dried oregano
- ½ tsp dried mint
- 1 lb (454 g) low-sodium boneless, skinless chicken breasts, cut into 1-inch pieces

- 1 cup cherry tomatoes
- 1 small yellow summer squash

Directions:

1. Whisk lemon juice, olive oil, parsley, oregano, and mint in a large bowl.
2. Add chicken and stir to coat. Let stand for 10 minutes at room temperature.
3. Alternating items, thread chicken, tomatoes, and squash onto 8 bamboo or metal skewers that fit in an air fryer. Brush with marinade.
4. Air fry kebabs at 380°F (193°C) for about 15 minutes, brushing once with any remaining marinade until the chicken reaches an internal temperature of 165°F (74°C) on a meat thermometer. Discard any remaining marinade. Serve immediately.

Nutrition:

- **Calories:** 164
- **Carbohydrates:** 4 g
- **Fat:** 4 g
- **Protein:** 27 g

150. Tandoori Chicken

Preparation Time: 5 minutes

Cooking Time: 23 minutes

Servings: 4

Ingredients:

- $^2/_3$ cup plain low-fat yogurt
- 2 tbsp freshly squeezed lemon juice
- 2 tsp curry powder
- ½ tsp ground cinnamon
- 2 garlic cloves, minced
- 2 tsp olive oil
- 4 (5-oz / 142-g) low-sodium boneless, skinless chicken breasts

Directions:

1. Whisk yogurt, lemon juice, curry powder, cinnamon, garlic, and olive oil.
2. With a sharp knife, cut thin slashes into the chicken. Add it to the yogurt mixture and

turn to coat. Let stand for 10 minutes at room temperature. You can also prepare this ahead of time and marinate chicken in the refrigerator for up to 24 hours.

3. Remove the chicken from the marinade and shake off any excess liquid. Discard any remaining marinade.
4. Roast the chicken at 360°F (182°C) for 10 minutes. With tongs, carefully turn each piece. Roast for 8 to 13 minutes more, or until the chicken reaches an internal temperature of 165°F (74°C) on a meat thermometer. Serve immediately.

Nutrition:

- **Calories:** 198
- **Carbohydrates:** 4 g
- **Fat:** 5 g
- **Protein:** 33 g

151. Baked Lemon Pepper Chicken Drumsticks

Preparation Time: 5 minutes

Cooking Time: 22 minutes

Servings: 4

Ingredients:

- Olive oil spray
- 6 chicken drumsticks
- 1 tsp lemon pepper
- ½ tsp salt
- ½ tsp granulated garlic
- ½ tsp onion powder

Directions:

1. Spray chicken with olive oil and spray the air fryer basket, or line it with parchment paper.
2. In a small bowl, combine lemon pepper, salt, garlic, and onion powder.
3. Place chicken in a prepared air fryer basket, and sprinkle with half of the seasoning mixture.
4. Bake at 370°F (188°C) for 10 minutes.

5. Flip drumsticks, spray them with more olive oil and sprinkle with the remaining seasoning.
6. Place chicken back in the air fryer, bake for an additional 12 minutes and serve.
7. Chicken is done when the internal temperature reaches 180°F (82°C), and juices run clear. It should look slightly crisp on the outside.

Nutrition:

- **Calories:** 195
- **Carbohydrates:** 1 g
- **Fat:** 11 g
- **Protein:** 23 g

152. Balsamic Glazed Chicken

Preparation Time: 5 minutes

Cooking Time: 22 minutes

Servings: 4

Ingredients:

Glaze:

- 1 tbsp olive oil
- 2 tsp balsamic vinegar
- 1 tsp minced garlic
- 1 tsp honey
- ½ tsp cornstarch
- ¼ tsp salt
- ¼ tsp pepper

Chicken:

- Olive oil spray
- 4 bone-in chicken thighs
- 2 tsp granulated garlic, divided
- 1 tsp salt, divided
- ½ tsp pepper, divided
- ¼ tsp onion powder, divided

Directions:

Make glaze:

1. Whisk together olive oil, balsamic vinegar, garlic, honey, cornstarch, salt, and pepper in a small bowl. Set aside.

Make chicken:

2. Spray chicken and air fryer basket with olive oil.
3. Place chicken in the air fryer basket, and sprinkle with about half garlic, salt, pepper, and onion powder.
4. Bake at 380°F (193°C) for 10 minutes.
5. Remove chicken and flip pieces. Spray it with more olive oil, and sprinkle with the remaining seasoning.
6. Place chicken back in the air fryer and bake for an additional 10 minutes.
7. Remove chicken, and brush with prepared glaze. Bake for an additional 2 minutes, or until sauce is sticky and caramelized, and serve.

Nutrition:

- **Calories:** 263
- **Carbohydrates:** 3 g
- **Fat:** 11 g
- **Protein:** 38 g

153. Harissa Roasted Cornish Game Hens

Preparation Time: 9 minutes

Cooking Time: 22 minutes

Servings: 4

Ingredients:

Harissa:

- ½ cup olive oil
- 6 cloves garlic, minced
- 2 tbsp smoked paprika
- 1 tbsp ground coriander
- 1 tbsp ground cumin
- 1 tsp ground caraway
- 1 tsp salt
- ½ to 1 tsp cayenne pepper

Hens:

- ½ cup yogurt
- 2 cornish game hens, any giblets removed and split in half lengthwise

Directions:

Make harissa:

1. In a medium microwave-safe bowl, combine oil, garlic, paprika, coriander, cumin, caraway, salt, and cayenne. Microwave on high for 1 minute, stirring halfway through cooking time. (You can also heat this on the stovetop until the oil is hot and bubbling. Or, if you must use your air fryer for everything, air fry it in the air fryer at 350° F (177° C) for 5 to 6 minutes, or until the paste is heated through.)

For hens:

2. In a small bowl, combine 1 to 2 tbsp harissa and yogurt. Whisk until well combined. Place hen halves in a resealable plastic bag and pour marinade over. Seal the bag and massage until all of the pieces are thoroughly coated. Marinate at room temperature for 30 minutes or in the refrigerator for up to 24 hours.
3. Arrange hen halves in a single layer in the air fryer basket. (If you have a smaller air fryer, you may have to cook this in two batches.) Roast at 400°F (204°C) for 20 minutes. Use a meat thermometer to ensure game hens have reached an internal temperature of 165°F (74°C).

Nutrition:

- **Calories:** 412
- **Carbohydrates:** 5 g
- **Fat:** 32 g
- **Protein:** 26 g

154. Honey Mustard Turkey Breast

Preparation Time: 5 minutes

Cooking Time: 31 minutes

Servings: 4

Ingredients:

- ¼ cup honey
- ¼ cup olive oil
- 1 tbsp Dijon mustard
- 1 tbsp butter, melted
- 2 tsp minced garlic
- 1 tsp salt
- ½ tsp pepper
- 2 ½ lb (1.1 kg) boneless turkey breast

Directions:

1. In a small bowl, whisk well to combine honey, olive oil, Dijon mustard, butter, garlic, salt, and pepper.
2. Place turkey breast in the air fryer basket, and brush with honey mixture.
3. Bake at 400°F (204°C) for 20 minutes.
4. Remove turkey breast, brush it with more of the honey mixture, and bake for an additional 10 minutes, until golden.
5. Let turkey rest for 5 to 10 minutes before slicing and serving.

Nutrition:

- **Calories:** 526
- **Carbohydrates:** 18 g
- **Fat:** 22 g
- **Protein:** 64 g

155. Cheese Chicken Fries

Preparation Time: 13 minutes

Cooking Time: 28 minutes

Servings: 4

Ingredients:

- 1 lb chicken (Cut into lengthy strips)

For marinade:

- 1 tbsp olive oil
- 1 tsp mixed herbs
- ½ sp red pepper flakes
- ⅛ tsp salt
- 1 tbsp lemon juice

For garnish:

- A cupful of cheddar cheese (melted)

Directions:

1. Combine all marinade ingredients into an empty bowl and mix properly.
2. Place chicken strips into a pot and boil them till partly cooked, then dip them into the prepared marinade and set aside.
3. Put Air Fryer on and preheat for about 5 minutes at a temperature of 300°F. Put chicken strips into the frying basket of the Air Fryer and cover the basket.
4. Then set the temperature at 220°F for 20 minutes. Toss fries about 3 to 4 times during the cooking process to ensure even cooking.
5. Just before cooking time elapses, spread coriander leaves on the fries. Then take fries out, serving them with melted cheese as a topping.

Nutrition:

- **Calories:** 242
- **Carbohydrates:** 3 g
- **Fat:** 6 g
- **Protein:** 23 g

156.   All Herbs and Cheese Chicken

Preparation Time: 8 minutes

Cooking Time: 26 minutes

Servings: 4

Ingredients:

- 4 chicken, skinless, boneless, halved
- 2 tsp tarragon, chopped
- 1 tbsp parsley, chopped
- 1 tbsp dill, chopped
- ½ goat cheese, crumbled, reduced-fat
- 3 tbsp basil, chopped
- 2 tsp lemon zest, grated
- ½ tsp salt
- ¼ tsp pepper

Directions:

1. Preheat Air Fryer to 350°F.
2. Coat herbed chicken with little cooking oil.
3. In a bowl, combine lemon zest, tarragon, parsley, dill, and basil. Add goat cheese to

the mixture. Set aside some of the herb mixtures.
4. Make a small pocket in the chicken breast. Each pocket should be filled with the herb mixture. Secure the pocket using a toothpick. Season with salt, pepper, and herb mixture.
5. Cook chicken for 10 minutes on each side. Serve.

Nutrition:

- **Calories:** 180
- **Carbohydrates:** 20 g
- **Fat:** 3.5 g
- **Protein:** 18 g

157.   Air Fried Beef Tenderloin with Vegetables

Preparation Time: 8 minutes

Cooking Time: 23 minutes

Servings: 4

Ingredients:

- 2 ½ lb beef tenderloin
- ½ green bell pepper, julienned
- ½ red bell pepper, deseeded, ribbed, julienned
- 2 tbsp light soy sauce
- 1 cup almond flour, finely milled
- ¼ tsp black pepper
- Pinch of stevia
- Pinch of salt
- 3 tbsp olive oil
- 2 onions, julienned
- 1 banana chili, julienned
- Pinch of salt
- Pinch of black pepper

Directions:

1. Preheat Air Fryer to 330°F.
2. Put beef tenderloin in a food-safe bag together with marinade ingredients. Massage beef and shake well. Put inside refrigerator for 1 hour or overnight.

3. Layer beef in the Air fryer basket. Fry for 5 minutes on each side or until beef is lightly brown in color. Repeat the step until all meat is cooked.

4. Meanwhile, sauté peppers and onion in a pan for 2 minutes. Spoon veggies on a plate. Serve with beef tenderloin.

Nutrition:

- **Calories:** 89.4
- **Carbohydrates:** 0.5 g
- **Fat:** 3.5 g
- **Protein:** 13.2 g

158.   Butter-Lemon Air Fried Chicken

Preparation Time: 6 minutes

Cooking Time: 21 minutes

Servings: 3

Ingredients:

- 4 pieces of corn on the cob, halved into equal portions
- ¼ tbsp butter
- $1/16$ tsp fine salt
- 1 5 to 5.6 lb whole chicken, skinless
- 1 large garlic head, keep whole
- 1 lemon, half sliced into equal wedges, remaining half squeezed but reserve spent lemon rind
- ½ tbsp smoky paprika powder
- ¼ tsp garlic powder
- 2 tbsp butter, low fat
- ¼ tsp turmeric powder
- ¼ tsp onion powder
- $1/8$ tsp stevia
- 1 tbsp salt
- $1/8$ tsp black pepper
- 2 tbsp olive oil

Directions:

1. Preheat Air Fryer to 360°F.
2. Find a spot under the chicken breast where skin and meat can be gently separated.

Using your fingers, rub butter under the skin, right up to creases.

3. Mix black pepper, stevia, garlic powder, kosher salt, olive oil, onion powder, paprika powder, and turmeric powder in a bowl. Rub the mixture vigorously all over the chicken, including the inside cavity.

4. Stuff garlic and spent lemon rind inside the chicken.

5. Place chicken breast side down into the Air Fryer basket. Cook for 60 minutes. Flip the chicken right side up midway through cooking.

6. Remove the chicken from the basket. Place on a platter. Drizzle in half of the lemon juice.

7. Loosely tent chicken with a sheet of aluminum foil. Rest for at least 10 minutes before discarding the garlic head and lemon rind. Carve into desired pieces.

8. Drizzle in the remaining lemon juice.

9. For corn, rub butter all over the corn. Wrap each piece individually in sheets of aluminum foil.

10. Place these in the Air Fryer basket at the same heat setting. Cook for 6 minutes.

11. Remove corn from the basket. Cool slightly before removing the aluminum foil. Season corn with a small amount of salt just before serving.

12. Serve the desired amount of chicken with corn on the side.

Nutrition:

- **Calories:** 260
- **Carbohydrates:** 2.0 g
- **Fat:** 14.5 g
- **Protein:** 54.9 g

159.   Flavored Pork Chops

Preparation Time: 9 minutes

Cooking Time: 38 minutes

Servings: 2

Ingredients:

- 3 cloves of ground garlic

- 2 tbsp olive oil
- 1 tbsp marinade
- 4 thawed pork chops

Directions:

1. Mix cloves of ground garlic, marinade, and oil. Then apply this mixture to chops.
2. Put chops in the air fryer at 360°C for 35 minutes.

Nutrition:

- **Calories:** 118
- **Carbohydrates:** 0 g
- **Fat:** 3.41 g
- **Protein:** 22 g

160.   Potatoes with Loin and Cheese

Preparation Time: 5 minutes

Cooking Time: 32 minutes

Servings: 4

Ingredients:

- 1kg potatoes
- 1 large onion
- 1 piece of roasted loin
- 3 tbsp Extra virgin olive oil
- ½ tsp Salt
- 1 tsp Ground pepper
- 2 tbsp Grated cheese

Directions:

1. Peel potatoes, cut cane, wash, and dry.
2. Put salt and add some threads of oil; we bind well.
3. Pass potatoes to the basket of the air fryer and select 180°C for 20 minutes.
4. Meanwhile, put some extra virgin olive oil in a pan, add peeled onion, and cut into julienne.
5. When the onion is transparent, add chopped loin.
6. Sauté well and pepper.
7. Put potatoes on a baking sheet.
8. Add onion with loin.
9. Cover with a layer of grated cheese.

10. Bake a little until the cheese takes heat and melts.

Nutrition:

- **Calories:** 382
- **Carbohydrates:** 2 g
- **Fat:** 3.41 g
- **Protein:** 2.9 g

161.   Spiced Pork Chops

Preparation Time: 8 minutes

Cooking Time: 11 minutes

Servings: 2

Ingredients:

- 2 boneless pork chops
- 15 ml vegetable oil
- 25 g dark brown sugar, packaged
- 6 g Hungarian paprika
- 2 g ground mustard
- 2 g freshly pepper
- 3 g onion powder
- 3 g garlic powder
- Salt and pepper to taste

Directions:

1. Preheat the air fryer for a few minutes at 180°C.
2. Cover pork chops with oil.
3. Put all spices and season pork chops abundantly, almost as if you were making them breaded.
4. Place pork chops in the preheated air fryer.
5. Select Steak, and set the time to 10 minutes.
6. Remove pork chops when it has finished cooking. Let it stand for 5 minutes and serve.

Nutrition:

- **Calories:** 118
- **Carbohydrates:** 0.3 g
- **Fat:** 6.85 g
- **Protein:** 13.12 g

162. Pork Rind

Preparation Time: 9 minutes

Cooking Time: 62 minutes

Servings: 4

Ingredients:

- 1 kg pork rinds
- Salt
- ½ tsp black pepper coffee

Directions:

1. Preheat the air fryer. Set time of 5 minutes and temperature to 200°C.
2. Cut bacon into cubes (1 finger wide).
3. Season with salt and a pinch of pepper.
4. Place in the basket of the air fryer. Set the time to 45 minutes and press the power button.
5. Shake the basket every 10 minutes so that the pork rinds stay golden brown equally.
6. Once they are ready, drain them a little on a paper towel, so they stay dry. Transfer to a plate and serve.

Nutrition:

- **Calories:** 282
- **Carbohydrates:** 0.3 g
- **Fat:** 23.41 g
- **Protein:** 16.59 g

163. Meatloaf Reboot

Preparation Time: 13 minutes

Cooking Time: 8 minutes

Servings: 2

Ingredients:

- 4 slices of leftover meatloaf, cut about 1-inch thick.
- Cooking spray

Directions:

1. Preheat your air fryer to 350°F.
2. Spray each side of the meatloaf slices with cooking spray. Add slices to the air fryer and cook for about 9 to 10 minutes.

3. Don't turn slices halfway through the cooking cycle, because they may break apart. Instead, keep them on one side to cook to ensure they stay together

Nutrition:

- **Calories:** 201
- **Carbohydrates:** 9.6 g
- **Fat:** 5 g
- **Protein:** 38 g

164. Mediterranean Lamb Meatballs

Preparation Time: 5 minutes

Cooking Time: 42 minutes

Servings: 4

Ingredients:

- 454 g ground lamb
- 3 cloves garlic, minced
- 5 g salt
- 1 g black pepper
- 2 g mint, freshly chopped
- 2 g ground cumin
- 3 ml hot sauce
- 1 g chili powder
- 1 scallion, chopped
- 8 g parsley, finely chopped
- 15 ml fresh lemon juice
- 2 g lemon zest
- 10 ml olive oil

Directions:

1. Mix lamb, garlic, salt, pepper, mint, cumin, hot sauce, chili powder, scallion, parsley, lemon juice, and lemon zest until well combined.
2. Create balls with lamb mixture and cool for 30 minutes.
3. Select Preheat in the air fryer and press Start/Pause.
4. Cover meatballs with olive oil and place them in the preheated fryer.
5. Select the Steak set the time to 10 minutes, and press Start/Pause.

Nutrition:

- **Calories:** 282
- **Carbohydrates:** 0.1 g
- **Fat:** 23.41 g
- **Protein:** 16.59 g

165. Potatoes with Bacon, Onion, and Cheese

Preparation Time: 6 minutes

Cooking Time: 18 minutes

Servings: 4

Ingredients:

- 200 g potatoes
- 150 g bacon
- 1 onion
- 2 Slices of cheese
- 4 tsp Extra virgin olive oil
- Salt as required

Directions:

1. Peel the potatoes, cut them into thin slices and wash them well.
2. Drain and dry potatoes, and put salt and a few strands of extra virgin olive oil.
3. Stir well and place in the basket of the air fryer.
4. Cut onion into julienne, put a little oil, and stir, place on potatoes.
5. Finally, put sliced bacon on the onion.
6. Take the basket to the air fryer and select 20 minutes, 180°C.
7. From time to time, remove the basket.
8. Take all contents of the basket to a source and when it is still hot, place slices of cheese on top.
9. You can let the heat of potatoes melt cheese, or you can gratin a few minutes in the oven.

Nutrition:

- **Calories:** 120
- **Carbohydrates:** 1 g
- **Fat:** 3.41 g
- **Protein:** 20.99 g

166. Herbed Pork Ribs

Preparation Time: 6 minutes

Cooking Time: 81 minutes

Servings: 4

Ingredients:

- 500 g pork ribs
- A pinch of Provencal herbs
- Salt and Ground pepper to taste
- Oil as desired

Directions:

1. Put ribs in a bowl and add some oil, Provencal herbs, salt, and ground pepper.
2. Stir well and leave in the fridge for at least 1 hour.
3. Put ribs in the air fryer basket and select 200°C for 20 minutes.
4. From time to time, shake the basket and remove the ribs.

Nutrition:

- **Calories:** 296
- **Carbohydrates:** 6 g
- **Fat:** 3.41 g
- **Protein:** 29 g

167. Chicken Fingers

Preparation Time: 15 minutes

Cooking Time: 22 minutes

Servings: 4

Ingredients:

- 2 tsp red pepper flakes
- 1 lb boneless skinless chicken breasts (cut into strips)
- 2 cupsful dry breadcrumbs
- 2 tsp oregano

For marinade:

- 2 tsp salt
- 6 tbsp corn flour
- 1 ½ tbsp ginger-garlic paste
- 1 tsp black pepper

- 4 tbsp fresh lemon juice
- 1 tsp chili powder
- 5 eggs

Directions:

1. Put all ingredients required for the marinade into a bowl and mix adequately. Put stripped chicken breasts into a bowl and refrigerate overnight to marinate sufficiently.
2. Now combine 1 tsp red pepper flakes, 2 tsp oregano, and 2 cups breadcrumbs in an empty bowl and mix properly. Coat marinated chicken strips in breadcrumb mix and cover with a food wrap till ready to cook.
3. Switch on your Air Fryer and preheat at a temperature of 160°F for a time frame of 5 minutes. Then put the chicken strips into the basket and close it. Allow chicken strips to cook for a further 15 minutes at the same temperature, tossing them properly at intervals to ensure an even fry.
4. Dish into plates and serve.

Nutrition:

- **Calories:** 142
- **Carbohydrates:** 3 g
- **Fat:** 5 g
- **Protein:** 23 g

168. Salted Biscuit Pie Turkey Chops

Preparation Time: 10 minutes

Cooking Time: 30 minutes

Servings: 4

Ingredients:

- 8 large turkey chops
- 300 g crackers
- 2 eggs
- 4 tbsp Extra virgin olive oil
- ½ tsp Salt
- 2 tsp Ground pepper

Directions:

1. Put turkey chops on the work table, and salt and pepper.
2. Beat eggs in a bowl.
3. Crush cookies in Thermo mix with a few turbo strokes until they are made grit, or you can crush them with the blender.
4. Put cookies in a bowl.
5. Pass chops through the beaten egg and then passed them through crushed cookies. Press well, so the empanada is perfect.
6. Paint the empanada with a silicone brush and extra virgin olive oil.
7. Put chops in the air fryer's basket; not all will enter. They will be done in batches.
8. Select 200°F, 15 minutes.
9. When you have all chops made, serve.

Nutrition:

- **Calories:** 126
- **Carbohydrates:** 0 g
- **Fat:** 6 g
- **Protein:** 18 g

169. Crispy Chicken Fillets

Preparation Time: 12 minutes

Cooking Time: 18 minutes

Servings: 3

Ingredients:

- 2 tbsp vegetable oil
- 2 large eggs (whisked)
- 13 oz chicken fillets
- 9 tbsp breadcrumbs
- 1 tsp freshly pepper
- 3 ½ oz all-purpose flour
- ½ tsp kitchen salt

Directions:

1. Turn on your Air Fryer and preheat to 340°F.
2. Then add kitchen salt, pepper, and vegetable oil to the breadcrumbs and combine by mixing them totally.
3. Get two shallow bowls, and transfer whisked eggs into one and all-purpose

flour into the other. Dip chicken into a bowl with flour, dust chicken to get rid of surplus flour, and then dip flour-coated chicken into whisked eggs. Coat each fillet completely with breadcrumbs subsequently.

4. Take out the fry basket and lay chicken fillets inside.
5. Cook fillets for 12 minutes, set up the heat to 400°F, and continue cooking for an additional 5 minutes until fillets turn golden.

Nutrition:

- **Calories:** 142
- **Carbohydrates:** 3 g
- **Fat:** 5 g
- **Protein:** 23 g

Chapter 8. Dessert Recipes

170. Tasty Banana Cake

Preparation Time: 40 minutes

Cooking Time: 30 minutes

Servings: 4

Ingredients:

- 1 tbsp butter, soft
- 1 egg
- $1/3$ cup brown sugar
- 2 tbsp honey
- 1 banana
- 1 cup white flour
- 1 tbsp baking powder
- ½ tbsp cinnamon powder
- Cooking spray

Directions:

1. Spurt cake pan with cooking spray.
2. Mix in butter with honey, sugar, banana, cinnamon, egg, flour, and baking powder in a bowl, then beat.
3. Empty mix in a cake pan with cooking spray, put it into the air fryer and cook at 350°F for 30 minutes.
4. Allow for cooling and slice.

5. Serve.

Nutrition:

- **Calories:** 145
- **Carbohydrates:** 9 g
- **Fat:** 16 g
- **Protein:** 4 g

171. Simple Cheesecake

Preparation Time: 25 minutes

Cooking Time: 26 minutes

Servings: 15

Ingredients:

- 1 lb cream cheese
- ½ tbsp vanilla extract
- 2 eggs
- 4 tbsp sugar
- 1 cup graham crackers
- 2 tbsp butter

Directions:

1. Mix in butter with crackers in a bowl.
2. Compress crackers blend to the bottom cake pan, put into the air fryer, and cook at 350°F for 4 minutes.
3. Mix cream cheese with sugar, vanilla, and egg in a bowl and beat properly.
4. Sprinkle filling on the crackers crust and cook the cheesecake in the air fryer at 310°F for 15 minutes.
5. Keep cake in the fridge for 3 hours, slice.
6. Serve.

Nutrition:

- **Calories:** 149
- **Carbohydrates:** 3 g
- **Fat:** 11 g
- **Protein:** 9 g

172. Bread Pudding

Preparation Time: 10 minutes

Cooking Time: 33 minutes

Servings: 4

Ingredients:

- 6 glazed doughnuts
- 1 cup cherries
- 4 egg yolks
- 1 ½ cup whipping cream
- ½ cup raisins
- ¼ cup sugar
- ½ cup chocolate chips.

Directions:

1. Mix in cherries with whipping cream and egg in a bowl, then turn properly.
2. Mix in raisins with chocolate chips, sugar, and doughnuts in a bowl, then stir.
3. Mix 2 mixtures, pour into an oiled pan, then into the air fryer, and cook at 310°F for 1 hour.
4. Cool pudding before cutting.
5. Serve.

Nutrition:

- **Calories:** 139
- **Carbohydrates:** 7 g
- **Fat:** 11 g
- **Protein:** 14 g

173. Bread Dough and Amaretto Dessert

Preparation Time: 22 minutes

Cooking Time: 42 minutes

Servings: 12

Ingredients:

- 1 lb bread dough
- 1 cup sugar
- ½ cup butter
- 1 cup heavy cream
- 12 oz chocolate chips
- 2 tbsp amaretto liqueur

Directions:

1. Turn the dough, cut it into 20 slices and cut each piece into halves.

2. Sweep dough pieces with spray sugar and butter, put them into the air fryer's basket and cook them at 350°F for 5 minutes. Turn them and cook for 3 minutes still. Move to a platter.
3. Melt heavy cream in a pan over medium heat, put chocolate chips and turn until they melt.
4. Put in liqueur, turn and move to a bowl.
5. Serve bread dippers with sauce.

Nutrition:

- **Calories:** 165
- **Carbohydrates:** 9 g
- **Fat:** 11 g
- **Protein:** 27 g

174. Wrapped Pears

Preparation Time: 10 minutes

Cooking Time: 16 minutes

Servings: 4

Ingredients:

- 4 puff pastry sheets
- 14 oz vanilla custard
- 2 pears
- 1 egg
- ½ tbsp cinnamon powder
- 2 tbsp sugar

Directions:

1. Put wisp pastry slices on a flat surface and add a spoonful of vanilla custard at the center of each. Add pear halves and wrap.
2. Sweep pears with egg, cinnamon, and spray sugar, put into the air fryer's basket, and cook at 320°F for 15 minutes.
3. Split parcels on plates.
4. Serve.

Nutrition:

- **Calories:** 169
- **Carbohydrates:** 5 g
- **Fat:** 19 g
- **Protein:** 4 g

175.   Air Fried Bananas

Preparation Time: 10 minutes

Cooking Time: 14 minutes

Servings: 4

Ingredients:

- 3 tbsp butter
- 2 eggs
- 8 bananas
- ½ cup corn flour
- 3 tbsp cinnamon sugar
- 1 cup panko

Directions:

1. Warm up a pan with butter over medium heat, put panko, turn and cook for 4 minutes, then move to a bowl.
2. Spin each in flour, panko, and egg blend, assemble them in the air fryer's basket, grime with cinnamon sugar, and cook at 280°F for 10 minutes.
3. Serve immediately.

Nutrition:

- **Calories:** 166
- **Carbohydrates:** 9 g
- **Fat:** 11 g
- **Protein:** 4 g

176.   Cocoa Cake

Preparation Time: 10 minutes

Cooking Time: 22 minutes

Servings: 6

Ingredients:

- 4 oz butter
- 3 eggs
- 3 oz sugar
- 1 tbsp cocoa powder
- 3 oz flour
- ½ tbsp lemon juice

Directions:

1. Mix in 1 tbsp butter with cocoa powder in a bowl and beat.

2. Mix in the rest of the butter with eggs, flour, sugar, and lemon juice in another bowl, blend properly and move half into a cake pan
3. Put half of the cocoa blend, spread, and add the rest of the butter layer and crest with the remaining cocoa.
4. Put into the air fryer and cook at 360°F for 17 minutes.
5. Allow cooling before slicing.
6. Serve.

Nutrition:

- **Calories:** 139
- **Carbohydrates:** 2 g
- **Fat:** 11 g
- **Protein:** 4 g

177.   Apple Bread

Preparation Time: 10 minutes

Cooking Time: 46 minutes

Servings: 6

Ingredients:

- 3 cups apples
- 1 cup sugar
- 2 eggs
- 1 tbsp apple pie spice
- 2 cups white flour
- 1 tbsp baking powder
- 1 stick butter
- 1 cup water

Directions:

1. Mix in egg with 1 butter stick, sugar, and apple pie spice, then turn using the mixer.
2. Put apples and turn properly.
3. Mix baking powder with flour in another bowl and turn.
4. Blend 2 mixtures, turn, and move it to spring form pan.
5. Get spring form pan into the air fryer and cook at 320°F for 40 minutes
6. Slice.
7. Serve.

Nutrition:

- **Calories:** 144
- **Carbohydrates:** 2 g
- **Fat:** 16 g
- **Protein:** 9 g

178.   Banana Bread

Preparation Time: 10 minutes

Cooking Time: 42 minutes

Servings: 6

Ingredients:

- ¾ cup sugar
- ⅓ cup butter
- 1 tbsp vanilla extract
- 1 egg
- 2 bananas
- 1 tbsp baking powder
- 1 ½ cups flour
- ½ tbsp baking soda
- ⅓ cup milk
- 1 ½ tbsp cream of tartar
- Cooking spray

Directions:

1. Mix in milk with cream of tartar, vanilla, egg, sugar, bananas, and butter in a bowl and turn whole.
2. Mix in flour with baking soda and baking powder.
3. Blend 2 mixtures, turn properly, move into the oiled pan with cooking spray, put into the air fryer, and cook at 320°F for 40 minutes.
4. Remove bread, allow to cool, and slice.
5. Serve.

Nutrition:

- **Calories:** 184
- **Carbohydrates:** 5 g
- **Fat:** 14 g
- **Protein:** 4 g

179.   Mini Lava Cakes

Preparation Time: 10 minutes

Cooking Time: 26 minutes

Servings: 3

Ingredients:

- 1 egg
- 4 tbsp sugar
- 2 tbsp olive oil
- 4 tbsp milk
- 4 tbsp flour
- 1 tbsp cocoa powder
- ½ tbsp baking powder
- ½ tbsp orange zest
- ½ tsp salt

Directions:

1. Mix in egg with sugar, flour, salt, oil, milk, orange zest, baking powder, and cocoa powder, and turn properly. Move it to oiled ramekins.
2. Put ramekins in the air fryer and cook at 320°F for 20 minutes.
3. Serve warm.

Nutrition:

- **Calories:** 165
- **Carbohydrates:** 2 g
- **Fat:** 18 g
- **Protein:** 4 g

180.   Crispy Apples

Preparation Time: 10 minutes

Cooking Time: 30 minutes

Servings: 4

Ingredients:

- 2 tbsp cinnamon powder
- 5 apples
- ½ tbsp nutmeg powder
- 1 tbsp maple syrup
- ½ cup water
- 4 tbsp butter
- ¼ cup flour
- ¾ cup oats
- ¼ cup brown sugar
- ½ tsp salt

Directions:

1. Put apples in a pan and put nutmeg, maple syrup, cinnamon, and water.
2. Mix in butter with flour, sugar, salt, and oat, turn, put a spoonful of the blend over apples, get into the air fryer and cook at 350°F for 10 minutes.
3. Serve while warm.

Nutrition:

- **Calories:** 169
- **Carbohydrates:** 2 g
- **Fat:** 17 g
- **Protein:** 2 g

181.   Ginger Cheesecake

Preparation Time: 2 hours and 30 minutes

Cooking Time: 36 minutes

Servings: 6

Ingredients:

- 2 tbsp butter
- ½ cup ginger cookies
- 16 oz cream cheese
- 2 eggs
- ½ cup sugar
- 1 tbsp rum
- ½ tbsp vanilla extract
- ½ tbsp nutmeg

Directions:

1. Spread pan with butter and sprinkle cookie crumbs on the bottom.
2. Whisk cream cheese with rum, vanilla, nutmeg, sugar, and eggs, beat properly, and sprinkle with cookie crumbs.
3. Put in the air fryer and cook at 340°F for 20 minutes.
4. Allow the cheesecake to cool in the fridge for 2 hours before slicing.
5. Serve.

Nutrition:

- **Calories:** 195
- **Carbohydrates:** 2 g
- **Fat:** 18 g
- **Protein:** 4 g

182.   Cocoa Cookies

Preparation Time: 10 minutes

Cooking Time: 39 minutes

Servings: 12

Ingredients:

- 6 oz coconut oil
- 6 eggs
- 3 oz cocoa powder
- 2 tbsp vanilla
- ½ tbsp baking powder
- 4 oz cream cheese
- 5 tbsp sugar

Directions:

1. Mix in eggs with coconut oil, baking powder, cocoa powder, cream cheese, vanilla, and sugar in a blender and sway, and turn using a mixer.
2. Get it into a lined baking dish and into the fryer at 320°F and bake for 14 minutes.
3. Split the cookie sheet into rectangles.
4. Serve.

Nutrition:

- **Calories:** 185
- **Carbohydrates:** 6 g
- **Fat:** 19 g
- **Protein:** 4 g

183.   Special Brownies

Preparation Time: 10 minutes

Cooking Time: 38 minutes

Servings: 4

Ingredients:

- 1 egg
- ⅓ cup cocoa powder
- ⅓ cup sugar
- 7 tbsp butter
- ½ tbsp vanilla extract
- ¼ cup white flour
- ¼ cup walnuts
- ½ tbsp baking powder

- 1 tbsp peanut butter

Directions:

1. Warm pan with 6 tbsp butter and sugar over medium heat, turn and cook for 5 minutes, move to a bowl, put salt, egg, cocoa powder, vanilla extract, walnuts, baking powder, and flour, turn mix properly and into a pan.
2. Mix peanut butter with 1 tbsp butter in a bowl, heat in microwave for some seconds, turn properly and sprinkle brownies blend over.
3. Put in the air fryer and bake at 320°F for 17 minutes.
4. Allow brownies to cool and cut.
5. Serve.

Nutrition:

- **Calories:** 129
- **Carbohydrates:** 8 g
- **Fat:** 11 g
- **Protein:** 2 g

184. Blueberry Scones

Preparation Time: 20 minutes

Cooking Time: 49 minutes

Servings: 10

Ingredients:

- 1 cup white flour
- 1 cup blueberries
- 2 eggs
- ½ cup heavy cream
- ½ cup butter
- 5 tbsp sugar
- 2 tbsp vanilla extract
- 2 tbsp baking powder
- ½ tsp salt

Directions:

1. Mix in flour, baking powder, salt, and blueberries in a bowl and turn.
2. Mix heavy cream with vanilla extract, sugar, butter, and eggs, and turn properly.

3. Blend 2 mixtures, squeeze till dough is ready, obtain 10 triangles from the mix, put on a baking sheet in the air fryer, and cook them at 320°F for 10 minutes.
4. Serve cold.

Nutrition:

- **Calories:** 195
- **Carbohydrates:** 8 g
- **Fat:** 16 g
- **Protein:** 4 g

185. Chocolate Cookies

Preparation Time: 10 minutes

Cooking Time: 26 minutes

Servings: 12

Ingredients:

- 1 tbsp vanilla extract
- ½ cup butter
- 1 egg
- 4 tbsp sugar
- 2 cups flour
- ½ cup unsweetened chocolate chips

Directions:

1. Warm pan with butter over medium heat, turn and cook for 1 minute.
2. Mix in egg with sugar and vanilla extract in a bowl and turn properly.
3. Put flour, melted butter, and half of the chocolate chips and turn.
4. Move to a pan, sprinkle remaining chocolate chips over, put in the fryer at 330°F, and bake for 25 minutes.
5. Serve slices when cold.

Nutrition:

- **Calories:** 147
- **Carbohydrates:** 4 g
- **Fat:** 20 g
- **Protein:** 3 g

186. Tasty Orange Cake

Preparation Time: 42 minutes

Cooking Time: 30 minutes

Servings: 12

Ingredients:

- 6 eggs
- 1 orange
- 1 tbsp vanilla extract
- 1 tbsp baking powder
- 9 oz flour
- 2 oz sugar + 2 tbsp
- 2 tbsp orange zest
- 4 oz cream cheese
- 4 oz yogurt

Directions:

1. Hump the orange in a food processor properly.
2. Put 2 tbsp sugar, flour, vanilla extract, and baking powder and throb properly.
3. Move mix into 2 spring-form pans, put in the fryer, and cook at 330°F for 16 minutes.
4. Mix in cream cheese with yogurt and orange zest and the rest of the sugar in a bowl and turn properly.
5. Put one cake layer on a plate, half of the cream cheese blend, then the other cake layer, and the remaining cream cheese blend.
6. Properly rub and slice.
7. Serve.

Nutrition:

- **Calories:** 175
- **Carbohydrates:** 9 g
- **Fat:** 21 g
- **Protein:** 4 g

187.   Macaroons

Preparation Time: 10 minutes

Cooking Time: 8 minutes

Servings: 20

Ingredients:

- 2 tbsp stevia
- 4 egg whites
- 2 cups coconut
- 1 tbsp vanilla extract

Directions:

1. Mix in egg whites with stevia in a bowl and whisk using the mixer.
2. Put the coconut and vanilla extract, beat again, get small balls out of the mix, put in the air fryer, and cook at 340°F for 8 minutes.
3. Serve cold.

Nutrition:

- **Calories:** 172
- **Carbohydrates:** 7 g
- **Fat:** 11 g
- **Protein:** 3 g

188.   Lime Cheesecake

Preparation Time: 4 hours and 14 minutes

Cooking Time: 30 minutes

Servings: 10

Ingredients:

- 2 tbsp butter
- 2 tbsp sugar
- 4 oz flour
- ¼ cup coconut

For filling:

- 1 lb cream cheese
- Zest from 1 lime
- Juice from 1 lime
- 2 cups hot water
- 2 sachets of lime jelly

Directions:

1. Mix coconut with flour, sugar, and butter in a bowl, turn properly and compress the mixture to the bottom of the pan.
2. Get hot water in a bowl, put jelly sachets, and turn them till it melts.
3. Get cream cheese in a bowl, put the lime juice, zest and jelly and beat properly.
4. Get mix on the crust, rub, put in the air fryer, and cook at 300°F for 4 minutes.

5. Cool in fridge for 4 hours
6. Serve.

Nutrition:

- **Calories:** 199
- **Carbohydrates:** 8 g
- **Fat:** 11 g
- **Protein:** 5 g

189.   Strawberry Cobbler

Preparation Time: 35 minutes

Cooking Time: 23 minutes

Servings: 6

Ingredients:

- ¾ cup sugar
- 6 cups strawberries
- $1/_8$ tsp baking powder
- 1 tbsp lemon juice
- ½ cup flour
- A pinch of baking soda
- ½ cup water
- 3 ½ tbsp olive oil
- Cooking spray

Directions:

1. Mix in strawberries with half of the sugar, put lemon juice, spray some flour in a bowl, beat, and turn into a baking dish and oil with cooking spray.
2. Mix in flour with baking powder, the rest of the sugar, and soda, and turn properly.
3. Put olive oil and blend with your hands.
4. Get ½ cup water and sprinkle over strawberries.
5. Put in the fryer at 355°F and roast for 25 minutes.
6. Allow the cobbler to cool, and slice.
7. Serve.

Nutrition:

- **Calories:** 185
- **Carbohydrates:** 9 g
- **Fat:** 11 g
- **Protein:** 4 g

190.   Air Fried Sugar-Free Chocolate Soufflé

Preparation Time: 15 minutes

Cooking Time: 18 minutes

Servings: 2

Ingredients:

- $1/_3$ cup milk
- 2 tbsp butter soft to melt
- 1 tbsp flour
- 2 tbsp Splenda
- 1 egg yolk
- ¼ cup sugar-free chocolate chips
- 2 egg whites
- ½ tsp cream of tartar
- ½ tsp vanilla extract

Directions:

1. Grease ramekins with spray oil or softened butter.
2. Sprinkle with any sugar alternative, and make sure to cover them.
3. Let the air fryer preheat to 325 to 330°F
4. Melt chocolate in a microwave-safe bowl. Mix every 30 seconds until fully melted.
5. Or use a double boiler method.
6. Melt 1 ½ tbsp butter over low-medium heat in a small-sized skillet.
7. Once the butter has melted, then whisk in flour. Keep whisking until thickened. Then turn the heat off.
8. Add egg whites with cream of tartar, with the whisk attachment, in a stand mixer, and mix until peaks form.
9. Meanwhile, combine ingredients in a melted chocolate bowl, add flour mixture and melted butter to the chocolate, and blend. Add in vanilla extract, egg yolks, and the remaining sugar alternative.
10. Fold egg white peaks gently with ingredients into a bowl.
11. Add mix into ramekins about ¾ full of 5-oz ramekins
12. Let it bake for 12 to 14 minutes, or until done.

Nutrition:

- **Calories:** 288
- **Carbohydrates:** 5 g
- **Protein:** 6 g
- **Fat:** 24 g

191. Sugar-Free Air Fried Carrot Cake

Preparation Time: 14 minutes

Cooking Time: 41 minutes

Servings: 8

Ingredients:

- 1 ¼ cup all-purpose flour
- 1 tsp pumpkin pie spice
- 1 tsp baking powder
- ¾ cup Splenda
- 2 cups carrots–grated
- 2 eggs
- ½ tsp baking soda
- ¾ cup canola oil

Directions:

1. Let the air fryer preheat to 350°F. Spray the cake pan with oil spray.
2. And add flour over that.
3. Combine baking powder, flour, pumpkin pie spice, and baking soda in a bowl.
4. In another bowl, mix eggs, oil, and sugar alternative. Now combine dry to wet ingredients.
5. Add half of the dry ingredients first mix and the other half of the dry mixture.
6. Add in grated carrots.
7. Add cake batter to the greased cake pan.
8. Place the cake pan in the basket of the air fryer.
9. Let it Air fry for half an hour, but do not let the top too brown.
10. If the top is browning, add a piece of foil over the top of the cake.
11. Air fry it until a toothpick comes out clean, 35 to 40 minutes in total.
12. Let the cake cool down before serving.

Nutrition:

- **Calories:** 287
- **Carbohydrates:** 19 g
- **Protein:** 4 g
- **Fat:** 22 g

192. Sugar-Free Low-Carb Cheesecake Muffins

Preparation Time: 16 minutes

Cooking Time: 28 minutes

Servings: 18

Ingredients:

- ½ cup Splenda
- 1 ½ cream cheese
- 2 eggs
- 1 tsp vanilla extract
- Oil

Directions:

1. Let the oven preheat to 300°F.
2. Spray the muffin pan with oil.
3. Add sugar alternatives, vanilla extract and cream cheese in a bowl. Mix well
4. Add in eggs gently, one at a time. Do not over-mix batter.
5. Let it bake for 25 to 30 minutes, or until cooked.
6. Take them out from the air fryer and let them cool before adding frosting.
7. Serve and enjoy.

Nutrition:

- **Calories:** 93
- **Carbohydrates:** 1 g
- **Protein:** 2 g
- **Fat:** 9 g

193. Sugar-Free Air Fried Chocolate Donut Holes

Preparation Time: 15 minutes

Cooking Time: 16 minutes

Servings: 32

Ingredients:

- 6 tbsp Splenda

- 1 cup of any flour
- ½ tsp baking soda
- 6 tbsp unsweetened cocoa powder
- 3 tbsp butter
- 1 egg
- ½ tsp baking powder
- 2 tbsp unsweetened chocolate chopped
- ¼ cup plain yogurt

Directions:

1. Combine baking powder, soda, and flour in a large mixing bowl.
2. Then add in cocoa powder and sugar alternative.
3. In a mug or microwave-safe bowl, melt butter and unsweetened chocolate.
4. Mix every 15 seconds and make sure they melt together and combine well.
5. Set it aside to cool it down.
6. In that big mixing bowl from before, add yogurt and egg. Add in melted butter and chocolate mixture. Cover the bowl with plastic wrap and let it chill in the refrigerator for 30 minutes.
7. To make donut balls, take out the batter from the fridge.
8. With the help of a tablespoon, scoop out sufficient batter so a donut ball will form with your hands.
9. You can use oil on your hands if the dough is too sticky.
10. Spray oil on the air fryer basket, sprinkle with flour and let it preheat to 350°F.
11. Work in batches and add balls in one single layer.
12. Let it bake for 10 to 12 minutes until they are done. To check doneness, try a toothpick if it comes out clean.
13. Take it out from the air fryer, let it cool and serve hot or cold.

Nutrition:

- **Calories:** 22
- **Carbohydrates:** 1 g
- **Protein:** 1 g
- **Fat:** 2 g

194. Sugar-Free Low Carb Peanut Butter Cookies

Preparation Time: 16 minutes

Cooking Time: 8 minutes

Servings: 23

Ingredients:

- 1 cup all-natural 100% peanut butter
- 1 whisked egg
- 1 tsp liquid stevia drops
- 1 cup sugar alternative

Directions:

1. Mix all ingredients into a dough. Make 24 balls with your hands from the combined dough.
2. On a cookie sheet or cutting board, press dough balls with help of a fork to form a crisscross pattern.
3. Add six cookies to the air fryer basket in a single layer. Make sure cookies are separated from each other. Cook in batches.
4. Let them air-fry for 8 to 10 minutes at 325°F. Take the basket out from the air fryer.
5. Let cookies cool for 1 minute, then with care, take cookies out.
6. Keep baking the rest of the peanut butter cookies in batches.
7. Let them cool completely and serve.

Nutrition:

- **Calories:** 198
- **Carbohydrates:** 7 g
- **Protein:** 9 g
- **Fat:** 17 g

195. Air Fryer Blueberry Muffins

Preparation Time: 9 minutes

Cooking Time: 16 minutes

Servings: 8

Ingredients:

- ½ cup sugar alternative
- 1 ⅓ cup flour
- ⅓ cup oil
- 2 tsp baking powder
- ¼ tsp salt
- 1 egg
- ½ cup milk
- Eight muffin cups (foil) with paper liners or silicone baking cups
- ⅔ cup frozen and thawed blueberries, or fresh

Directions:

1. Let the air fryer preheat to 330°F.
2. In a large bowl, sift together baking powder, salt, sugar, and flour. Mix well
3. Add milk, oil, and egg into another bowl and mix it well.
4. To dry ingredients to the egg mix, mix until combined but do not over mix
5. Add blueberries carefully. Pour the mixture into muffin paper cups or muffin baking tray
6. Put four muffin cups in the air fryer basket, or add more if your basket's size is big.
7. Cook for 12 to 14 minutes, at 330°F, or until when touched lightly on the tops, it should spring back.
8. Cook the remaining muffins accordingly.
9. Take them out from the air fryer and let them cool before serving.

Nutrition:

- **Calories:** 213
- **Carbohydrates:** 13.2 g
- **Fat:** 10 g
- **Protein:** 9.7 g

196. Air Fryer Sugar-Free Lemon Slice & Bake Cookies

Preparation Time: 5 minutes

Cooking Time: 8 minutes

Servings: 24

Ingredients:

- ½ tsp salt
- ½ cup coconut flour
- ½ cup unsalted butter softened
- ½ tsp liquid vanilla stevia
- ½ cup Swerve granular sweetener
- 1 tbsp lemon juice
- ¼ tsp lemon extract, optional
- 2 egg yolks
- 2 tbsp baking soda

For icing:

- 3 tsp lemon juice
- ⅔ cup Swerve confectioner's sweetener

Directions:

1. In a stand mixer bowl, add baking soda, coconut flour, salt, and Swerve; mix until well combined
2. Then add butter (softened) to dry ingredients, and mix well. Add all remaining ingredients but do not add in yolks yet. Adjust the seasoning of lemon flavor and sweetness to your liking; add more if needed.
3. Add yolk and combine well.
4. Lay a big piece of plastic wrap on a flat surface, put the batter in the center, roll around the dough and make it into a log form, for almost 12 inches. Keep this log in the fridge for 2 to 3 hours or overnight, if possible.
5. Let the oven preheat to 325°F. Generously spray the air fryer basket, take the log out from the plastic wrap, only unwrap how much you want to use it, and keep the rest in the fridge.
6. Cut in ¼-inch cookies, place as many cookies in the air fryer basket in one single, and do not overcrowd the basket.
7. Bake for 3 to 5 minutes until the cookies' edges become brown. Let it cool in the basket for 2 minutes, then take it out from the basket. And let them cool on a wire rack.

8. Once all cookies are baked, pour icing over them. Serve and enjoy.

Nutrition:

- **Calories:** 66
- **Carbohydrates:** 2 g
- **Fat:** 6 g
- **Protein:** 1 g

197. Easy Air Fryer Brownies

Preparation Time: 9 minutes

Cooking Time: 8 minutes

Servings: 2

Ingredients:

- 2 tbsp baking chips
- $1/3$ cup almond flour
- 1 egg
- ½ tsp baking powder
- 3 tbsp powdered sweetener (sugar alternative)
- 2 tbsp cocoa powder (unsweetened)
- 2 tbsp chopped pecans
- 4 tbsp melted butter

Directions:

1. Let the air fryer preheat to 350°F
2. In a large bowl, add cocoa powder, almond flour, Swerve sugar substitute, and baking powder, and give it a good mix.
3. Add melted butter and crack an egg in dry ingredients.
4. Mix well until combined and smooth.
5. Fold in chopped pecans and baking chips.
6. Take two ramekins to grease them well with softened butter. Add batter to them.
7. Bake for 10 minutes. Make sure to place them as far from the heat source on top of the air fryer.
8. Take brownies out from the air fryer and let them cool for 5 minutes.
9. Serve with your favorite toppings, and enjoy.

Nutrition:

- **Calories:** 201
- **Carbohydrates:** 14.1 g
- **Fat:** 10.2 g
- **Protein:** 8.7 g

198. Air Fryer Thumbprint Cookies

Preparation Time: 15 minutes

Cooking Time: 8 minutes

Servings: 10

Ingredients:

- 1 tsp baking powder
- 1 cup almond flour
- 3 tbsp natural low-calorie sweetener
- 1 large egg
- 3 ½ tbsp raspberry (reduced-sugar) preserves
- 4 tbsp softened cream cheese

Directions:

1. Add egg, baking powder, flour, sweetener, and cream cheese in a large bowl, and mix well until a dough (wet) forms.
2. Chill dough in the fridge for almost 20 minutes, until dough is cool enough
3. And then form into balls.
4. Let the air fryer preheat to 400°F, and add parchment paper to the air fryer basket.
5. Make ten balls from the dough and put them in the prepared air fryer basket.
6. Make an indentation from your thumb in the center of every cookie with your clean hands. Add 1 tsp raspberry preserve in the thumb hole.
7. Bake in the air fryer for 7 minutes, or until light golden brown to your liking.
8. Let cookies cool completely on parchment paper for almost 15 minutes, or they will fall apart.
9. Serve with tea and enjoy.

Nutrition:

- **Calories:** 111.6
- **Carbohydrates:** 9.1 g
- **Protein:** 3.7 g

- **Fat:** 8.6 g

199. Air Fryer Apple Fritter

Preparation Time: 9 minutes

Cooking Time: 11 minutes

Servings: 3

Ingredients:

- ½ apple (pink lady apple or honey crisp) peeled, finely chopped
- ½ cup all-purpose flour
- 1 tsp baking powder
- ¼ tsp salt
- ½ tsp ground cinnamon
- 2 tbsp brown sugar or sugar alternative
- ⅛ tsp ground nutmeg
- 3 tbsp Greek yogurt (fat-free)
- 1 tsp butter

For glaze:

- 2 tbsp powdered sugar
- ½ tbsp water

Directions:

1. Add baking powder, nutmeg, brown sugar (or alternative), flour, cinnamon, and salt to a large mixing bowl. Mix it well,
2. With the help of a fork or cutter, slice butter until crumbly. It should look like wet sand.
3. Add chopped apple and coat well, then add fat-free Greek yogurt.
4. Keep stirring or tossing until everything is together and a crumbly dough forms.
5. Put dough on a clean surface and knead it into a ball form with your hands.
6. Flatten the dough in an oval shape about a half-inch thick. It is okay, even if it's not the perfect size or shape.
7. Spray the basket of the air fryer with cooking spray generously. Put the dough in air fry for 12 to 14 minutes at 375°F and cook until light golden brown.
8. For making the glaze, mix the ingredients and with help of a brush, pour over the apple fritter when it comes out from the air fryer.
9. Slice and serve after cooling for 5 minutes.

Nutrition:

- **Calories:** 200
- **Carbohydrates:** 14 g
- **Fat:** 12 g
- **Protein:** 9.8 g

200. Grain-Free Molten Lava Cakes

Preparation Time: 5 minutes

Cooking Time: 11 minutes

Servings: 2

Ingredients:

- 2 large eggs
- ½ cup chocolate chips, you can use dark chocolate
- 2 tbsp coconut flour
- 2 tbsp honey as a sugar substitute
- A dash of salt
- ½ tsp baking soda
- Butter and cocoa powder for (two small ramekins)
- ¼ cup butter or grass-fed butter

Directions:

1. Let the air fryer preheat to 370°F.
2. Grease ramekins with soft butter and sprinkle with cocoa powder. It will stick to butter. Turn ramekins upside down, so excess cocoa powder will fall out. Set it aside.
3. In a double boiler or microwave, safe bowl, melt butter and chocolate chips together and stir every 15 seconds. Make sure to mix well to combine.
4. In a large bowl, crack eggs and whisk with either honey or sugar, and mix well. Add baking soda, sea salt, and coconut flour. Gently fold everything.
5. Then add the melted chocolate chip and butter mixture to the egg, flour, and honey mixture. Mix well, so everything combines.

6. Pour batter into those two prepared ramekins.
7. Let them air fry for ten minutes. Then take them out from the air fryer and let them cool for 3 to 4 minutes.
8. When cool enough to handle, run a knife along the edges so the cake will out easier.
9. After flipping them upside down on a serving plate.
10. Top with mint leaves and coconut cream, raspberries, if you want. Serve right away and enjoy.

Nutrition:

- **Calories:** 217
- **Carbohydrates:** 14 g
- **Fat:** 12 g
- **Protein:** 9.9 g

201.   Tahini Oatmeal Chocolate Chunk Cookies

Preparation Time: 11 minutes

Cooking Time: 8 minutes

Servings: 8

Ingredients:

- $^1/_3$ cup tahini
- ¼ cup walnuts
- ¼ cup maple syrup
- ¼ cup chocolate chunks
- ¼ tsp alt
- 2 tbsp almond flour
- 1 tsp vanilla, optional
- 1 cup gluten-free oat flakes
- 1 tsp cinnamon, optional

Directions:

1. Let the air fryer preheat to 350°F.
2. Add maple syrup, cinnamon (if used), tahini, salt, and vanilla (if used) in a large bowl. Mix well, then add in walnuts, oat flakes, and almond meals. Then fold the chocolate chips gently.
3. Now that the mix is ready take a full tbsp of the mixture and separate it into 8 amounts.

Wet clean damp hands, press them on a baking tray or with a spatula.
4. Place four cookies or more, depending on your air fryer size, and line the air fryer basket with parchment paper in one single layer.
5. Let them cook for 5 to 6 minutes at 350°F, and air fry for more minutes if you like them crispy.

Nutrition:

- **Calories:** 185.5
- **Carbohydrates:** 18.5 g
- **Fat:** 11.2 g
- **Protein:** 12 g

202.   Eggless & Vegan Cake

Preparation Time: 5 minutes

Cooking Time: 18 minutes

Servings: 8

Ingredients:

- 2 tbsp olive oil
- ¼ cup all-purpose flour
- 2 tbsp cocoa powder
- $^1/_8$ tsp baking soda
- 3 tbsp sugar
- 1 tbsp warm water
- 3 tbsp milk
- 2 drops of vanilla extract, optional
- 4 raw almonds for decoration, roughly chopped, optional
- A pinch of salt

Directions:

1. Let the air fryer preheat to 190°C for at least 2 minutes.
2. Whisk sugar, milk, water, and oil until a smooth batter forms.
3. Now add salt, all-purpose flour, cocoa powder, and baking soda, sift them into wet ingredients, and mix to form a paste
4. Spray a four-inch baking pan with oil and pour batter into it. Then add chopped-up almonds on top of it.

5. Put the baking pan in the preheated air fryer. And cook for 10 minutes.
6. Check doneness with a toothpick. They are done if it comes out clean but may need another minute.
7. Take out from the air fryer.
8. Let it cool completely before slicing.
9. Serve and enjoy.

Nutrition:

- **Calories:** 120
- **Carbohydrates:** 18 g
- **Fat:** 8 g
- **Protein:** 2 g

203.   Berry Cheesecake

Preparation Time: 9 minutes

Cooking Time: 51 minutes

Servings: 8

Ingredients:

- ½ cup raspberries
- 2 blocks of softened cream cheese, 8 oz
- 1 tsp raspberry or vanilla extract
- ¼ cup strawberries
- 2 eggs
- ¼ cup blackberries
- 1 cup and 2 tbsp sugar alternative of confectioner sweetener

Directions:

1. In a big mixing bowl, whip sugar-alternative confectioner sweetener and cream cheese; mix and whip until smooth and creamy.
2. Then add in raspberry or vanilla extract and eggs; again, mix well.
3. In a food processor or a blender, pulse berries and fold into cream cheese mix with 2 extra tbsp of sweetener.
4. Take a spring from the pan and spray oil generously, pour in the mixture.
5. Put the pan in the air fryer, let it air fryer, and cook for ten minutes at 300°F. Lower the temperature to 400°F and cook for 40 minutes.

6. To check if it's done, shake it lightly. It is done if everything is set and the middle part is jiggled.
7. Take out from the air fryer and cool a bit before chilling in the fridge.
8. Keep in the fridge for 2 to 4 hours or as long as you have time.
9. Slice and serve, enjoy.

Nutrition:

- **Calories:** 225
- **Carbohydrates:** 18 g
- **Fat:** 17 g
- **Protein:** 12 g

204.   Banana Muffins in Air Fryer

Preparation Time: 9 minutes

Cooking Time: 11 minutes

Servings: 8

Ingredients:

Wet mix:

- 3 tbsp milk
- 1 tsp Nutella (it is optional)
- 4 Cavendish size, ripe bananas
- ½ cup sugar alternative
- 1 tsp vanilla essence
- 2 large eggs

Dry mix:

- 1 tsp baking powder
- 1 ¼ cup whole wheat flour
- 1 tsp baking soda
- 1 tsp cinnamon
- 2 tbsp cocoa powder, optional
- 1 tsp salt

Optional:

- 1 handful of chopped walnuts
- Fruits, dried slices
- Chocolate sprinkles

Directions:

1. With a fork, in a bowl, mash up bananas, add all wet ingredients to it, and mix well.
2. Sift all dry ingredients, so they combine well. Add into wet ingredients. Carefully fold both ingredients together. Do not over mix.
3. Then add in diced walnuts, slices of dried-up fruits, and chocolate sprinkles.
4. Let the air fryer preheat to 120°C
5. Add batter into muffin cups. Before that, spray them with oil generously.
6. Air fryer them for at least half an hour, or until a toothpick comes out clean
7. Take them out from the air fryer and let them cool down before serving.

Nutrition:

- **Calories:** 210
- **Carbohydrates:** 18 g
- **Fat:** 13 g
- **Protein:** 12 g

205. Apple Cider Vinegar Donuts

Preparation Time: 9 minutes

Cooking Time: 10 minutes

Servings: 8

Ingredients:

For muffins:

- 1 cup coconut flour
- 4 eggs, large
- 4 tbsp coconut oil, melted
- 1 tsp baking soda
- $2/3$ cup apple cider vinegar
- 1 tsp cinnamon
- 3 tbsp honey
- A pinch of salt

For drizzle:

- Coffee Syrup (turmeric pumpkin spice)

Directions:

1. Let the air fryer pre-heat to 350°F. Spray oil on a baking tray, spray a generous amount of grease with melted coconut oil
2. In a large bowl, add apple cider vinegar, honey, melted coconut oil, and salt mix well, then crack eggs and whisk it all together.
3. Sift coconut flour, baking soda, and cinnamon in another bowl so the dry ingredients will combine well.
4. Now add wet ingredients to dry ingredients until completely combined. Do not worry if the batter is kind of wet.
5. Pour batter into the prepared donut baking pan. And add batter into cavities. With the help of your hands, spread the batter in the cavity evenly.
6. Let it bake for 10 or 8 minutes at 350°F, or until light golden brown.
7. Make sure halfway through cooking if they are not getting too brown. With a toothpick, check to see if the donuts are cooked, and the toothpick comes out clean.
8. Take them out from the oven and let them cool for at least 10 minutes to harden up, then remove otherwise. They will fall apart since they are very tender.
9. Before serving, drizzle with coffee syrup (turmeric pumpkin spice).
10. Serve right away and enjoy.

Nutrition:

- **Calories:** 179
- **Carbohydrates:** 9 g
- **Fat:** 11.2 g
- **Protein:** 5 g

206. Strawberry Vanilla Cupcake

Preparation Time: 38 minutes

Cooking Time: 16 minutes

Servings: 4

Ingredients:

- 1 lb whole wheat flour
- 4 tbsp strawberry sauce

- ¾ of a cupful of icing sugar
- 2 large eggs
- 2 strawberries (halved each)
- 2 tsp beetroot powder
- 2 tsp vanilla extract
- 1 tsp cocoa powder
- 5 oz peanut butter
- ½ lb cold butter (for icing)
- Some colorful chocolates (ground)

Directions:

1. Put whole wheat flour, 2 large eggs, 5 oz peanut butter, 1 tsp cocoa, 2 tsp beet powder, and ¾ cup icing sugar into an electric mixer and mix properly. Transfer the batter formed into cupcake molds.
2. Turn on Air Fryer and set the cooking temperature to 355°F to preheat for 5 minutes. Put the cupcake mold in the air fryer and decrease the cooking temperature to 335°F. Leave to bake for 15 minutes.
3. Take out cupcakes afterward, and set them aside to cool for 8 minutes.
4. Combine ½ lb cold butter, 2 tsp vanilla extract, and icing sugar in an electric mixer and keep whisking them together till an even texture is achieved.
5. Layer this whisked sugar and vanilla mix on top of the cupcakes and scatter some strawberry sauce and colored chocolates as well.
6. Serve cupcakes with half of the strawberry as toppings.

Nutrition:

- **Calories:** 189
- **Carbohydrates:** 6 g
- **Fat:** 11.2 g
- **Protein:** 5 g

207. Sugary Cinnamon Rolls

Preparation Time: 9 minutes

Cooking Time: 31 minutes

Servings: 8

Ingredients:

For rolls:

- 2 tbsp butter (dissolved)
- ½ a tsp cinnamon powder
- 2 tbsp all-purpose flour
- 2 ½ oz brown sugar
- A tube of cooled croissants
- Salt

For glaze:

- 1 tbsp soy milk
- ¼ cupful cream cheese (softened)
- 4 oz icing sugar

Directions:

For rolls:

1. Line the base of the Air Fryer with baking paper and grease with butter. In an empty bowl, put in 2 tbsp butter, ½ tsp cinnamon, some kosher salt, and 2 ½ oz brown sugar, and mix properly until the texture is fluffy.
2. Spread some flour on a neat surface, then place and roll out the croissants to form one cylindrical croissant. Fasten seams by pinching jointly and folding in the middle. Mold the croissant roll into an 8×6-inch rectangle. Coat the entire surface of the dough with butter. Beginning at a lengthy end, roll the dough up similar to a jelly roll, and then cut the dough diagonally into 8 parts.
3. Take out the fry basket and lay croissant cuts, with the cut portion facing upwards, and then space them uniformly.
4. Turn on Air Fryer and set the cooking temperature to 345°F. Leave rolls to cook till they turn slightly golden; typically taking 12 minutes.
5. For making the glaze, pour ¼ cup cream cheese, 4 oz icing sugar, and 1 tbsp soy milk into a small bowl. If the glaze is too dense, then add more milk to lighten the glaze.
6. Cover the top of the rolls with glaze before serving.

Nutrition:

- **Calories:** 188
- **Carbohydrates:** 9 g
- **Fat:** 12 g
- **Protein:** 5 g

208.   Tasty Chocolate Muffins

Preparation Time: 15 minutes

Cooking Time: 18 minutes

Servings: 12

Ingredients:

- 1 cupful superfine sugar
- 6 tbsp milk
- 2 cupsful self-rising flour
- 1 large egg
- ½ a cupful of butter
- ¼ cupful cocoa powder
- ½ tsp vanilla essence

Directions:

1. Turn Air Fryer on and set the temperature to 350°F to preheat. Put self-rising flour, ¼ cup cocoa, and 1 cup superfine sugar into an empty mixing bowl. Then put in ½ cup butter and stir until the mixture is coarsely loose.
2. Break the egg into another bowl and pour in 6 tbsp milk and vanilla essence.
3. Transfer the egg and milk mixture into the bowl containing cocoa and flour mix, and stir it in properly. Add in a little water to lighten the batter if too dense.
4. Scoop some batter into muffin cases, and lay them inside the air fryer. Leave cupcakes to cook at a temperature of 345°F for 10 minutes, and then cook at 330°F for 5 minutes.
5. Allow muffins to cool off before serving.

Nutrition:

- **Calories:** 203
- **Carbohydrates:** 8 g

- **Fat:** 14 g
- **Protein:** 5 g

209.   Delicious Chocolate Chip Cookie

Preparation Time: 15 minutes

Cooking Time: 18 minutes

Servings: 6

Ingredients:

- ½ cupful of butter (softened)
- ½ cupful of white sugar
- ½ cupful brown sugar
- 2 eggs
- 1 tsp vanilla
- ½ tsp baking soda
- ¼ tsp table salt
- 1 ½ cupsful all-purpose flour
- 1 cupful of chocolate chips

Directions:

1. Turn on the air fryer and adjust the cooking temperature to 350°F to preheat for 5 minutes. Get two heat-resistant pans of suitable size for the Air Fryer and grease them.
2. Combine softened butter, ½ cup brown sugar, and ½ cup brown sugar in a large bowl. Then introduce vanilla and 2 eggs into the same pan. Also, add ½ tsp baking soda, 1 ½ cup all-purpose flour, and ¼ tsp salt. Finally, add chocolate morsels.
3. Transfer the mixed dough into each of greased pans and push the formed dough down the base of each heat-resistant pan. In sequence, bake each for 10 minutes till slightly browned round ends.

Nutrition:

- **Calories:** 197
- **Carbohydrates:** 9 g
- **Fat:** 17 g
- **Protein:** 2 g

Conclusion

A stationary lifestyle is one in which you sit a large portion of the day and embrace minimal physical activity. The connection between inactive conduct and the danger of diabetes is simply demonstrated. Physical exercise expands the insulin affectability of cells when you exercise; less insulin is required to empower your blood glucose to enter your cells. Numerous physical movement types decrease blood glucose levels in pre-diabetic grown-ups who are stout or overweight, counting vigorous exercise, quality preparing, and high-power stretch preparation.

One study of pre-diabetics showed that high-force exercise expanded insulin effectively by 85%, while tolerable extreme exercise expanded it by over half. However, this impact just occurred when they worked out. To improve insulin reaction in pre-diabetics, they expected to consume in any event 2,000 calories per week through exercise. That isn't too difficult to think about doing if you set your focus on it. Try to locate a physical action you appreciate and usually embrace and stick to it as long as possible.

Quitting smoking, other than tumors of the lung, breast, prostate, colon, throat, and stomach-related tract, just as emphysema and coronary illness, has proven connections between smoking (and introduction to recycled smoke) and type 2 diabetes. Smoking builds the danger of diabetes by 44% in regular smokers and 61% in overwhelming smokers (more than 20 cigarettes every day), contrasted with non-smokers as per a meta-investigation of a few studies that together secured more than one million smokers.

Quitting smoking diminishes this hazard after some time, but not right away. Most individuals who develop type 2 diabetes are overweight or hefty. Also, individuals with pre-diabetes will generally have visceral fat, i.e., they haul their excess weight around their center and stomach organs, for example, the liver. Studies have demonstrated that increased visceral fat advances insulin opposition, expanding the danger of diabetes significantly. This hazard can be diminished by shedding pounds, particularly around the center. One investigation of more than 1,000 individuals found that for each kilogram (2.2 lbs.) they lost; their danger of diabetes was decreased by 16%. This examination found that the most extreme hazard decrease was 96%, i.e., a loss of 6 kilograms (13.2 lbs.).

There are numerous sound ways of shedding pounds through exercise and dieting. You have numerous dietary alternatives to browse, such as Mediterranean, paleo, low-carb, and vegan. The best, maybe, is the Beating-Diabetes diet. Reduce the fat in your diet. As you know, the primary driver of type 2 diabetes is fat sticking up the receptors in your muscle cells, so the insulin can't open the cell films to permit glucose to enter. The "fix" is to unblock the receptors.

As you are pre-diabetic, fat is now starting to gum up the receptors. You can unblock the receptors by limiting the fat you ingest in your diet. To limit the fat you eat, make sure that under 10% of the content in any food you eat originates from fat (read the marks) and reduce your utilization of meat, eggs, and dairy items as reasonably as possible, and center around foods dependent on plants (products of the soil). You can't change your past conduct, your age, or even your qualities. However, you can manage to improve your lifestyle, what you eat and drink, and how you take care of yourself.

Using an Air Fryer can be hard at first. Following our tips and tricks in this book will cook like a pro in no time! We have listed all sorts of recipes in this book so that you can ensure that you never run out of gas while trying to make your favorite foods again! Make sure to read through the whole book so that you can get everything right. There's something about Air-fryers. Once you think about it, they're kind of like a meal in a bit, without the hassle of actually cooking. One thing you need to do is to place a slice of bread or your favorite dish (or even a sandwich!), place it in the appliance, and wait for it to cook.

Air fryers are convenient because they can be used at all hours. You can use them for cooking your favorite dish for dinner while you're getting ready or for a quick snack. You can even use them for cooking large meals such as breakfast foods or ethnic dishes overnight and saving yourself from having to clean up after dinner. When you're using an Air-fryer, though, be careful about what foods you use. Some foods are difficult or impossible to fry when using an Air-fryer, so avoid using certain ingredients such as breaded chicken and pancakes with syrup or butter. There may be some other things you want to avoid, too, so be sure to check out our article on the diabetic Air-fryer cookbook.

The Diabetic Air-Fryer Cookbook provides a complete guide to using your air-fryer for the first time. In this part, you will have all the information you need to know about using your Air-fryer. It covers some basic information as well as advanced techniques. This cookbook is designed to teach you some of the basics about how to use your Air-fryer, allowing you to enjoy all of its great features. We start with a shortlist of rules and tips that will help you make sure you are using your Air-fryer correctly. You'll be able to cook healthy food every time with little effort and save money in the process! Make healthier choices without sacrifice by using this innovative and easy-to-use appliance!

This book will allow you to master the art of air frying and make your favorite meals completely pain-free and healthier than ever. One of the finest ways to cook healthy food in a microwave is to use the air frying method. It involves cooking with steam, without oil or fats. This means that your kitchen will be free from a "fried" smell, and you can have a healthier diet. This cookbook's contents will help you learn exactly how to do this by following step-by-step instructions that will be written for you without confusing words or often-used terms. We will teach you how to prepare and cook delicious and nutritious dishes quickly and easily when cooked using an Air Fryer. You can make breakfast, lunch, dinner, snacks, and desserts, so easily using this method. You will be able to prepare them in under 30 minutes without storing or freezing the ingredients because the foods are not fried at all.

It is just one of the key things that you can get from this book. Along with the "how-to" instructions, you will also receive helpful tips and tricks to help you when cooking with an Air Fryer. I am very glad that you have come this far, I have spent a lot of time writing this book, and now I kindly ask you to help me, I would really appreciate your positive review on Amazon, your reviews are much more important than you imagine!

Meal Plan

This is an example meal plan, the combination of all the recipes in the book can apply to a 1900-day meal plan.

30 days meal plan	Breakfast	Lunch	Dinner	Dessert
Day 1	Air fryer meatballs in tomato sauce	Salmon cakes in the air fryer	Fried pork chops	Tasty banana cake
Day 2	Chicken fried spring rolls	Coconut shrimp	Pork liver	Simple cheesecake
Day 3	Air-fried cinnamon biscuit bite	Crispy fish sticks in the air fryer	Air fried meatloaf	Bread pudding
Day 4	Macaroni cheese toast	Honey-glazed salmon	Pork tenderloin	Bread dough and amaretto dessert
Day 5	Mushroom and cheese frittata	Basil-parmesan crusted salmon	Pork bondiola chop	Wrapped pears
Day 6	Air-fried flaxseed French toast sticks with berries	Cajun shrimp in the air fryer	Mustard lamb loin chops	Air fried bananas
Day 7	Cinnamon and cheese pancake	Crispy air fryer fish	Herbed lamb chops	Cocoa cake
Day 8	Low-carb white egg and spinach frittata	Air fryer lemon cod	Za'atar lamb loin chops	Apple bread
Day 9	Scallion sandwich	Air fryer salmon fillets	Pesto-coated rack of lamb	Banana bread
Day 10	Lean lamb and turkey meatballs with yogurt	Tuna sandwich	Spiced lamb steaks	Mini lava cakes
Day 11	Air fried eggs	Scrambled salmon egg	Steak	Crispy apples

Day 12	Cinnamon pancake	Air fryer fish & chips	Marinated loin potatoes	Ginger cheesecake
Day 13	Spinach and mushrooms omelet	Grilled salmon with lemon	Beef with mushrooms	Cocoa cookies
Day 14	All berries pancakes	Air-fried fish nuggets	Cheesy and crunchy Russian steaks	Special brownies
Day 15	Air-fried aubergine and tomato	Garlic rosemary grilled prawns	Roasted vegetable and chicken salad	Blueberry scones
Day 16	Quick fry chicken with cauliflower	Air-fried crumbed fish	Chicken satay	Chocolate cookies
Day 17	Air-fried artichoke hearts	Parmesan garlic-crusted salmon	Mini turkey meatloaves	Tasty orange cake
Day 18	Air-fryer onion strings	Air fryer salmon with maple soy glaze	Chicken fajitas with avocados	Macaroons
Day 19	Fried spinach	Air-fried Cajun salmon	Crispy buttermilk fried chicken	Lime cheesecake
Day 20	Air-fried zucchini flowers	Air fryer shrimp scampi	Garlicky chicken with creamer potatoes	Strawberry cobbler
Day 21	Garlic bread with cheese dip	Sesame seeds fish fillet	Baked chicken cordon bleu	Air-fried sugar-free chocolate soufflé
Day 22	Fried mixed veggies with avocado dip	Lemon pepper shrimp in the air fryer	Chicken tenders and vegetables	Sugar-free air-fried carrot cake
Day 23	Sweet potato crisps	Air-fried fish and chips	Greek chicken kebabs	Sugar-free low-carb cheesecake muffins
Day 24	Fried green tomatoes	Scallops and dill	Tandoori chicken	Sugar-free air-fried chocolate donut holes

Day 25	Mushroom frittata	Crispy fish sandwiches	Sweet potato lentil stew	Sugar-free low-carb peanut butter cookies
Day 26	Avocado taco fry	Lean pork and shrimp dumplings	Quick paella	Air fryer blueberry muffins
Day 27	Blueberry cream cheese sandwich	Pork on a blanket	Sea bass paella	Air fryer sugar-free lemon slice & bake cookies
Day 28	Tomatoes and cheese frittata	Vietnamese grilled pork	Brown rice, spinach, and tofu frittata	Easy air fryer brownies
Day 29	Egg white and flax crepes	Provencal's ribs	Beef and broccoli	Air fryer thumbprint cookies
Day 30	Bell pepper, salsa, and taco frittata	Air fryer beef steak kabobs with vegetables	Pineapple pudding	Air fryer apple fritter

Air Fryer Cooking Chart

Beef

Item	Temp (°F)	Time (mins)	Item	Temp (°F)	Time (mins)
Beef Eye Round Roast (4 lbs.)	400 °F	45 to 55	Meatballs (1-inch)	370 °F	7
Burger Patty (4 oz.)	370 °F	16 to 20	Meatballs (3-inch)	380 °F	10
Filet Mignon (8 oz.)	400 °F	18	Ribeye, bone-in (1-inch, 8 oz)	400 °F	10 to 15
Flank Steak (1.5 lbs.)	400 °F	12	Sirloin steaks (1-inch, 12 oz)	400 °F	9 to 14
Flank Steak (2 lbs.)	400 °F	20 to 28			

Chicken

Item	Temp (°F)	Time (mins)	Item	Temp (°F)	Time (mins)
Breasts, bone in (1 ¼ lb.)	370 °F	25	Legs, bone-in (1 ¾ lb.)	380 °F	30
Breasts, boneless (4 oz)	380 °F	12	Thighs, boneless (1 ½ lb.)	380 °F	18 to 20
Drumsticks (2 ½ lb.)	370 °F	20	Wings (2 lb.)	400 °F	12
Game Hen (halved 2 lb.)	390 °F	20	Whole Chicken	360 °F	75
Thighs, bone-in (2 lb.)	380 °F	22	Tenders	360 °F	8 to 10

Pork & Lamb

Item	Temp (°F)	Time (mins)	Item	Temp (°F)	Time (mins)
Bacon (regular)	400 °F	5 to 7	Pork Tenderloin	370 °F	15
Bacon (thick cut)	400 °F	6 to 10	Sausages	380 °F	15
Pork Loin (2 lb.)	360 °F	55	Lamb Loin Chops (1-inch thick)	400 °F	8 to 12
Pork Chops, bone in (1-inch, 6.5 oz)	400 °F	12	Rack of Lamb (1.5 – 2 lb.)	380 °F	22

Fish & Seafood

Item	Temp (°F)	Time (mins)	Item	Temp (°F)	Time (mins)
Calamari (8 oz)	400 °F	4	Tuna Steak	400 °F	7 to 10
Fish Fillet (1-inch, 8 oz)	400 °F	10	Scallops	400 °F	5 to 7
Salmon, fillet (6 oz)	380 °F	12	Shrimp	400 °F	5
Swordfish steak	400 °F	10			

Vegetables

INGREDIENT	AMOUNT	PREPARATION	OIL	TEMP	COOK TIME
Asparagus	2 bunches	Cut in half, trim stems	2 Tbsp	420°F	12-15 mins
Beets	1½ lbs	Peel, cut in ½-inch cubes	1Tbsp	390°F	28-30 mins
Bell peppers (for roasting)	4 peppers	Cut in quarters, remove seeds	1Tbsp	400°F	15-20 mins
Broccoli	1 large head	Cut in 1-2-inch florets	1Tbsp	400°F	15-20 mins
Brussels sprouts	1lb	Cut in half, remove stems	1Tbsp	425°F	15-20 mins
Carrots	1lb	Peel, cut in ¼-inch rounds	1 Tbsp	425°F	10-15 mins
Cauliflower	1 head	Cut in 1-2-inch florets	2 Tbsp	400°F	20-22 mins
Corn on the cob	7 ears	Whole ears, remove husks	1 Tbps	400°F	14-17 mins
Green beans	1 bag (12 oz)	Trim	1 Tbps	420°F	18-20 mins
Kale (for chips)	4 oz	Tear into pieces, remove stems	None	325°F	5-8 mins
Mushrooms	16 oz	Rinse, slice thinly	1 Tbps	390°F	25-30 mins
Potatoes, russet	1½ lbs	Cut in 1-inch wedges	1 Tbps	390°F	25-30 mins
Potatoes, russet	1lb	Hand-cut fries, soak 30 mins in cold water, then pat dry	¼ -3 Tbps	400°F	25-28 mins
Potatoes, sweet	1lb	Hand-cut fries, soak 30 mins in cold water, then pat dry	1 Tbps	400°F	25-28 mins
Zucchini	1lb	Cut in eighths lengthwise, then cut in half	1 Tbps	400°F	15-20 mins

Index of Recipes

Printed in Great Britain
by Amazon

10964008R00072